The Big Ninja Foodi Cookbook UK 2023

Simple and Fabulous Ninja Foodi Recipes on a Budget for Beginners With Easy to Follow Steps

Judy J. Smith

Contents

Introduction

Chapter 1: Breakfasts

Chapter 2: Poultry

Chapter 3: Fish and Seafood

Chapter 4: Beef, Pork and Lamb

Chapter 5: Vegetarian Mains

Chapter 6: Vegetables and Sides

Chapter 7: Family Favourites

Chapter 8: Desserts

Chapter 9: Soups and Stews

Introduction

If you ever have to get a pressure cooker, choose Uk Ninja Foodi Pressure Cooker. In this article, I'll tell you why it has to be this exact pressure cooker.

I have heard many stories about pressure cookers from family and friends. Still, I have never really had the experience of using one, thanks to the scary story of ugly explosions caused by a pressure cooker - I mean, it's gross having to scrape spaghetti off your ceiling.

However, when I got the Ninja pressure cooker, the cooker replaced my ugly expectations with satisfaction.

I visited a friend some months back. She was hosting a few friends and family for a weekend hang out. Everything was going great until, well, time started flying. The guests were hungry, and we still had to boil the chicken until tender before roasting. I had already started panicking - I mean, if you know me, it doesn't take long before I begin to panic. I was already asking questions, looking for how to speed up the cooking.

Then Sandra brought out one round, compact, stainless steel cooker coated with black enamel. I asked her what it was and heard it for the first time - The Ninja Foodi Pressure Cooker. 'But what does it do - really,' I asked further, and she said it was the magic instrument we needed.

I don't mean to sponsor the post or advertise, but I must tell you, the Ninja Foodi Pressure Cooker is a life changer. That one pot did the work of several other cookers; it is not just sweet talk. Though Sandra told me about that fateful day, I have also seen it. I have had my Ninja Pressure Cooker for about a year, and I use it to slow cook, pressure cook, steam, dehydrate, broil, keep foods warm, bake or roast, air fry until crisp, sous vide, sear, and sometimes, make yogurt. Count that - it should be 11 cooking functions. Some come with even more parts (up to 15), and some can be lesser (about 5 or 7 cooking functions-in-one cooker or even the 2-in-1 deluxe XL 8 qt. Pressure Cooker).

That's right! Sandra, that day used that single pot to broil the chicken until it was tender and then air-fried it again. We ate a delicious and healthy chicken piece that day in less time. For emphasis -

The cooker cut down cooking time by almost 70% of the original time we would have spent. Plus, we used less energy on her electrical cooking appliance - about 50% saved.

If I have convinced you about the pressure cooker, I have good news! I have more information about it. I decided to dig it up and reveal it so you can see how much I enjoy my Ninja Foodi Pressure Cooker and why. Read on below;

All about the Ninja Foodi, You Should Know

Here, I will explain what you need to know about the pressure cooker. Let's start with this. If you were like me, you would have checked online for so much information about the pressure cooker - but I will be honest. All you would see are sponsored posts for other Ninja Foodi cookers, the Pressure Cooker Air Fryer Combo, some posts from Amazon, and then on to Ninja Foodi Pressure Cooker Recipes you can try.

These pieces of information are helpful, but again, if you are like me, who spent hours looking for in-depth information on what the cooker was and how it differed from other types, then you need this. Below, I will explicitly explain what a Ninja Foodi Pressure Cooker is and how it differs from the different types of brands. I will also explain why I got so convinced that I knew there was no going back for me.

What is the Ninja Foodi Pressure Cooker?

The Ninja Foodi Pressure Cooker is an exceptional product manufactured by Ninja Foodi to cook food under high pressure. The product cuts cooking time by 70% and saves half of the gas or electrical energy you would have wasted cooking with another appliance. But more than all of this, the Foodi Pressure Cooker can serve multiple functions.

Great, right? But to help you understand the uniqueness of the product, let me go back a bit into Ninja Foodi - the brand itself. Ninja Foodi is a cooking equipment brand specializing in manufacturing and selling high-quality products. They have a unique air-fryer product, a steamer, a roaster, and so much more. But what is unique about this brand is that all their products - and I mean all are multifunctional.

Their slow cooker would also be able to steam, and their air-fryer can also bake - that's how they roll. However, for this Ninja Foodi Pressure Cooker series, the brand created various types for several customers. As I said, mine can do 11 things, while some can do 7, 5, 15, or just two things.

Why did I choose Ninja Foodi Pressure Cooker?

Do you still need to figure that out? Let me make it a list.

It is Multifunctional

Yes, this is my first reason. I can't help it, I'm not too fond of a cluttered kitchen, but I love to cook. Imagine having an air fryer on one side of the kitchen and then a deep fryer, an oven, a cooking pot, a yogurt maker, then a dehydrator - see where I am going with this?

With my Ninja Foodi 11-in-1 pressure cooker, I can do 11 things without needing to have 11 separate appliances in my kitchen. If this needs to be more convincing (maybe you have a pretty large kitchen), checkpoint number 2.

Quick Cooking Method

It takes me 6 minutes to air-fry a large chicken breast. Large! Yeah, you heard me. Depending on the heat level, it usually takes me 15 to 20 minutes, but with this magical pressure cooker, I get the food done in a jiffy. Plus, I can maintain speed for taste, flavor, and deliciousness. After I have finished cooking, all that and more will be packed into the chicken. It is like a wonder done to me - spending less time (30% of the original time) cooking anything.

The Cooker Saves Energy

I noticed that the electric pressure cooker has also benefited my electricity meter bill. I save more energy using the pressure cooker. Not only because it is fast and I spend less time cooking, but (this will take you a little bit to chemistry) the equipment traps pressure and cooking temperatures inside the pot. In an ordinary cooking pot, the electric stove needs to keep generating heat and pressure to balance the moisture level and required temperature to cook, but this doesn't happen for this pressure cooker.

Let me explain; you need to reach a minimum of 165oF to cook chicken (I love chicken). In a traditional cooking pot vs. Ninja Foodie pressure cooker, the temperature will keep escaping and drop the cooking temperature repeatedly. The cooking appliance would constantly utilize the energy generated from the stove to keep the temperature at 165. For this pressure cooker, the temperature is trapped in the pot, and you can cook at 165oF for as long as you want, while the electric stove can save energy.

Main Functions of Ninja Foodi

Quickly, here are the main functions the cooker has:

- Pressure Cook: This is the principal function of the Ninja Foodie Pressure Cooker vs. an instant cooking pot. Using this fast-pressure cooker, you can cut your cooking time by 70% and save energy. Ninja Foodi has a sealed cover to prevent heat and air from escaping. Hence the heat is trapped inside with water for quick cooking under high pressure. The pressure can be adjusted using the touch panel at the front of the device, and you can go as low or as high as you wish. Stay at the mid-point, though.

- Steam/Crisp: Though many people compare this process to air-frying, this is cooking that is done with a small amount of water (not oil). The Ninja Foodi Steam/Crisp Pressure Cooker is also designed to steam food until it becomes crisp on the outside and juicy on the inside. This process cuts down your cooking time by 40%

- Air-Fry/Stovetop: Air frying is where you cook food with little or no oil. The hot air is in charge of the cooking - at least a significant part of it. When it is done in a Ninja Foodi Air-fryer pressure pot, the cuisine becomes faster and worth the extra dollar - trust me.

Other functions I have tried with my pressure cooker are; proofing, steaming and baking, roasting, and slow cooking. You can also broil, boil(of course), dehydrate your food (made beef jerky just yesterday), sous vide, sear & saute, or keep foods warm before serving.

Guide on how to use the Ninja Foodi

There are five steps you need to take to use the product. Note that the steps might vary depending on what it is you wish to cook. However, you still need to follow these procedures to achieve a satisfying result after cooking. Here are the steps:

Step 1: Preheat

The first step is to heat the cooker before you do anything. Close the pot's lid and turn the heat to a low level just for the hot air to warm the device for a minute or two. Please don't set the temperature too high, nor keep it on for too long. Remember that it is just the pot you are 'cooking.'

Step 2: Pour Some Water

Whether you are cooking, frying, roasting, or steaming, a pressure cooker needs water to do its job. The amount of water you need might only vary. While some might need a small cup of water, other cooking methods, like broiling or steaming, would require you to add a lot of water.

Step 3: Choose the Cooking Method

The Ninja Foodi cooker comes with different lids for varying purposes. While there is an Air crisping lid used for air frying, there is also a pressure lid for pressure cooking. The cover also tells you about the other cooking functions available on the cooker. For instance, the air-crisping cap has buttons for dehydrating, broiling, roasting, baking, searing/sauteing, and so on. On the other hand, the lid for pressure cooking contains buttons for slow cooking, steaming, and keeping foods warm, among others.

Step 4: Put Your Food in + The Ingredients

Don't say, 'I will put my ingredients in later.' That might be a better idea. After you have chosen what it is you want to do and have kept the lid within reach, pour in your food and the ingredients alongside it. Let it all cook together; you'll be shocked by the results.

Step 5: Don't Forget the Inside Pot

Finally, before you close the pot with the lid, place the inside pot inside the cooker. I have always remembered the inside pot, but my research showed that the pressure cooking device overrides when the inside pot is not inside before cooking. Remember the final step to avoid this messy and risky situation.

If you have done all this, you can continue with your cooking. Set the desired time, and go back when your food is done. Allow the cooker to cool before opening the lid (to avoid getting burned), and there you go!

How to Clean & Maintain the Ninja Foodi Pressure Cooker

Let's talk a little about deep cleaning your pressure cooker. There are also steps here to make things easy. But note that this is not something you can do in a minute. You need to set time apart to deep clean your pressure cooker. Here are the steps for how to clean a pressure cooker.

- Pour one cup of hot water and lemon juice inside the pot.
- Pressure cook this mixture for about ten minutes.
- Be careful here: Quickly remove the pressure cooker lid, place the air-crisp lid back, and let it sit for another five minutes.
- (This process will allow the steam to cleanse and disinfect all the areas of the pot).
- Open the lid of the pot and pour away the mixture.
- Wash as you will with mild soap and warm water.
- You can either allow it to air-dry or wipe it clean with a soft microfiber cloth.
- Store it in a cool, dry place.

If you wish to clean it lightly, you only need a soft cloth, mild soap, and lukewarm water.

- Mix the soap and water inside a separate bowl.
- Then dip the cloth into the bowl to make it damp.
- Squeeze out any excess liquid from the fabric until it is simply damp, not wet and dripping.
- Use the cloth to wipe the surface of the pot and the inside pot as well.
- Rinse away with lukewarm water and air dry.
- Please keep it in a cool, dry place, away from direct sunlight.

So how often should you clean the Ninja Foodi Pressure Cooker? Every time after use! Do a light cleaning with mild soap and water after every use. You can then deep clean every two weeks (depending on the level of cooking you have been doing and the mess you might have made).

After each use, also ensure to wash the gasket and the lid. Use a damp cloth and mild soap to ensure the valve is also clean. Alternatively, you can clean the valve using a toothpick to remove food particles stuck in it.

But what about how to maintain your Ninja Foodi Pressure Cooker? Two rules exist. First, you should always turn it off when you are not cooking - leaving the lid open. Second, you should always keep your pressure cooker on a flat surface where it can stand stable. Please don't keep it close to the edge as well to prevent falling.

Pressure Cooking Tips

Before I round off, I will let you in on some tips I have gathered in the last year for using my Ninja Foodi 11-in-1 6.5-qt pressure cooker. These tips will also ensure you don't have spaghetti spilled all over your ceiling.

- Check the equipment before cooking to ensure everything is in the correct order. Inspect the rubber gasket and the rim of the pot. Also, ensure that you check the rubber ring that lines the cooker's lid (rubber gasket) to ensure it isn't dried out or cracked.
- Refrain from filling the cooker to the brim. You can always cook it twice (it's fast anyway) or buy a bigger pot. Mine is about 6.5L large. If you fill it to the brim, it can also break the pot's seal and damage it. This tip also works for foods that foam. If you are cooking spaghetti, cranberries, or any other food that tends to foam, pour a smaller amount inside the pot so that when the frothing does start during cooking, it will not go past the maximum food level in the cooker. Then, what is the maximum capacity to fill a pressure cooker? About half the space of the pot. If yours is like mine with a 6.5L capacity, fill your food to about 4L. Foods that froth should only reach about 2.5L
- Use enough water, sauce, or broth (at least ½ cup of the liquid for any food).
- Don't use the pressure cooking lid to fry. Just don't - it'll end badly.
- Release the pressure by allowing it to sit after removing the lid or by pouring cold water over the top before opening it.

With all of these tips, I can say that you can go ahead with your shoulders high, get yourself a nice Ninja Foodi Pressure Cooker and try some recipes. Good luck!

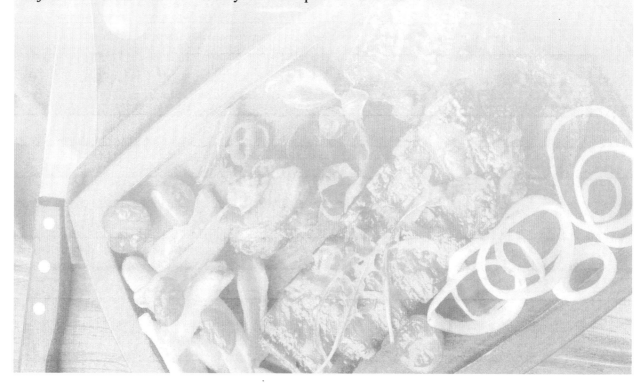

Blueberry Quinoa Granola

Air Crisp Function

Prep time: 5 mins

Cook time: 10 mins

Serves: 8

Ingredients:

- 50 g quinoa
- 130 ml water
- 2 tbsp honey
- 40 g chopped pecans
- 2 tbsp dried blueberries

Preparation Instructions:

1. Mix the quinoa and water in the inner pot.
2. Ensure the quinoa is covered with water.
3. Set the pressure function and put on high for one minute.
4. After one minute, allow the pot to naturally release for 5 minutes then manually release the remaining pressure.
5. Add in honey, pecans and dried blueberries.
6. Stir and mix well.
7. Cook for 8 -10 minutes at 200°C on Air Crisp feature.
8. Stir every few minutes.
9. Once dry, transfer to greaseproof paper to cool completely.

Breakfast Pizza

Air Fryer Function

Prep time: 10 mins

Cook time: 20 mins

Serves: 6 slices

Ingredients:

- 120 g plain flour
- 1 tsp baking powder
- 150 g fat-free greek yogurt
- 4 sausages
- 15 g granulated sugar
- ⅛ tsp salt
- 4 slices bacon
- 50 g grated cheese

Preparation Instructions:

1. Mix sugar, flour, and baking powder in a bowl followed by the greek yogurt.
2. Mix everything well together until crumbly.
3. Transfer dough onto a flat surface and mold it into a ball.
4. Using a rolling pin, make the dough into a circular shape of about 20 cm in diameter.
5. Spray the air fryer basket with spray oil.4
6. Brush the top of the dough with some milk.
7. On air fryer mode, cook for 10 minutes at 180°C. Flip and cook dough for a further 3 minutes.
8. As the dough crust is cooking, grill bacon and sausage until cooked.
9. Chop the bacon and sausage and distribute evenly across crust.
10. Top with grated cheese and return to air fryer for 3 - 5 minutes.
11. Cool on a wire rack for 3 minutes before eating!

Egg Bites

Air Crisp Function

Prep time: 5 mins
Cook time: 12 mins
Serves: 6

Ingredients:

- 6 eggs
- 60 ml low-fat milk
- 1 pepper
- 40 g onion, chopped
- Shredded ham
- Salt and Pepper

Preparation Instructions:

1. Beat eggs and milk together.
2. Add pepper, onion, and ham.
3. Season with salt and pepper.
4. Pour into a silicone egg mold, stopping each time just below the top of the mold.
5. Place the egg mold into the air crisp basket.
6. Cook at 180°C using the Air Crisp function for 8 - 12 minutes.
7. Remove from the basket and flip the mold to release the egg bites.

Bacon-wrapped Bagels with Mozzarella Cheese

Air Fryer Function

Prep time: 5 mins

Cook time: 10 mins

Serves: 2

Ingredients:

- 2 bagels
- 4 slices of bacon
- 100 g mozzarella cheese

Preparation Instructions:

1. Cut bagels in half.
2. Spread mozzarella cheese evenly between the two bagels.
3. Put two bagel halves together and wrap bacon around them to join them together.
4. Place in Air Fryer basket and cook at 190°C for 10 minutes.

Baked Oats with Banana and Blueberries

Air Fryer Function

Prep time: 5 mins

Cook time: 25 mins

Serves: 2

Ingredients:

- 2 bananas
- 80 g oats
- 1 tbsp chia seeds
- 240 ml milk
- 100 g blueberries
- 1 tbsp honey

Preparation Instructions:

1. Mash two bananas in your cooking dish.
2. Add oats, chia seeds milk, blueberries, and honey and mix well.
3. Cook in air fryer for 25 mins at 180°C.

Peach Crisp

Air Fryer Function

Prep time: 5 mins

Cook time: 30 mins

Ingredients:

- 375 g canned sliced peaches
- 3 tbsp brown sugar

- ¼ tsp cinnamon
- 20 g pecans, chopped
- 50 g butter
- 40 g oats
- 2 tbsp plain flour
- 1 tsp vanilla essence

Preparation Instructions:

1. Mix the peaches, sugar, and cinnamon and pour into a baking pan.
2. Place in air fryer and cook at 150°C for 20 minutes, turning the peaches halfway through.
3. Mix the rest of the ingredients in a bowl to make the crisp topping.
4. When peaches have cooked for 20 minutes, remove from air fryer and top with crisp topping.
5. Return to airfryer and cook for a further 10 minutes.
6. Allow to cool completely before serving.

Chocolate and Banana Croissant

Air Fryer Function

Prep time: 5 mins
Cook time: 5 mins
Serves: 1

Ingredients:

- 1 croissant
- ½ banana, sliced
- 1 tbsp chocolate spread

Preparation Instructions:

1. Cut slices, Hasselback style, along the croissant. Taking care not to cut the full way through.
2. Stuff the gaps with banana slices and chocolate spread.
3. Place in air fryer basket and cook for 5 minutes at 180°C or until the croissant is golden and crispy.

Strawberry Jam

Pressure Cooker Function

Prep time: 5 mins
Cook time: 1 hour
Serves: 12

Ingredients:

- 675 g strawberries
- 200 g sugar
- 3 tbsp lemon juice

Preparation Instructions:

1. Halve strawberries and remove greens.
2. Place strawberries in Ninja Foodi and mix with sugar and lemon juice.
3. Close lid and with no heat needed, allow to sit for 30 minutes.
4. Open lid and stir.
5. Close lid and using Pressure Cooker Function, cook on high for 1 minute.
6. When time is up, let pressure release naturally for 15 minutes and then manually release the pressure.
7. Mash the strawberries to your liking.
8. Using the Sear/Saute mode allow the mixture to come to a boil and allow it to boil for about 5 - 8 minutes.
9. Turn off Ninja Foodi and leave the jam to cool.

Air Fryer Bread

Air Fryer Function

Prep time: 1 hour 15 mins

Cook time: 12 mins

Serves: 10

Ingredients:

- 60 ml warm water
- 1 ½ sugar
- 1 ¼ tsp active dry yeast
- 60 ml warm milk
- ½ tsp salt
- 1 tbsp vegetable oil
- 185 g plain flour
- 1 tbsp butter

Preparation Instructions:

1. Whisk warm water, sugar and yeast together. Allow to sit for 5- 10 minutes until bubby and foamy.
2. Add milk and whisk again.
3. Add salt and vegetable oil and whisk.
4. Add flour 60 g at a time, pressing together until it forms a ball.
5. Prepare a floured surface for kneading.
6. Knead for about 5 minutes.
7. Place the dough in an oiled bowl, rolling it to cover all sides in oil.
8. Cover bowl with a thick cloth and allow to rise for about an hour.
9. When it has doubled in size, flatten the dough and knead for another minute.

10. Split dough in half and put into two greased loaf pans.
11. Cover with thick cloth for a further 30 minutes until about an inch above the man.
12. Cook in air fryer at 190°C for 12 minutes.

Yogurt

Pressure Cooker Function

Prep time: 10 mins

Cook time: 8 hours

Serves: 5

Ingredients:

- 650 ml milk
- 1 tbsp plain Greek yogurt
- 1 tbsp vanilla extract

Preparation Instructions:

1. Mix together the Greek yogurt with 240 ml of milk until smooth.
2. Pour the remaining milk into pressure cooked and stir well.
3. Add Vanilla.
4. Close lid but do not seal pressure.
5. Set pressure to normal and cook for 8 hours.
6. After this time, remove and allow to rest in fridge for at least 8 hours.

Rosemary Scones

Air Fryer Function

Prep time: 5 mins

Cook time: 15 mins

Serves: 2

Ingredients:

- 185 g plain flour
- 2 teaspoons sugar
- 1½ teaspoons baking powder
- ¼ teaspoon baking soda
- ½ teaspoon salt
- ⅛ teaspoon freshly ground black pepper
- ½ teaspoon lemon zest, finely grated
- 1½ teaspoons fresh rosemary, finely chopped
- 55 g plus 2 tablespoons unsalted butter, cold, and cut into pieces

• 120 ml plus 2 tablespoons well-shaken buttermilk, divided

Preparation Instructions:

1. Mix the sugar, baking powder, salt, baking soda, black pepper and flour in a medium bowl.
2. Add rosemary and lemon zest.
3. Blend the mixture to a crumb texture and then add the butter using a fork.
4. Stir in 120 ml plus 1 tablespoon of the buttermilk with a fork, and the mixture should be just moistened.
5. Press the dough and form it into a rough ball.
6. Lightly dust a clean work surface and your hands. Pat the dough and then continue to knead until it just comes together. Shape into a rectangle.
7. Then roll the dough into 1.5 cm thick with a lightly floured rolling pin.
8. Cut the dough crosswise into 3 portions and then cut each into 2 triangle-shaped scones.
9. Evenly arrange the scones on the baking pan, and brush them with the remaining buttermilk.
10. Place the baking pan in the air fryer, and Bake them at 200°C for 14 minutes.
11. When cooked, carefully remove it from the air fryer.

Egg in Avocado

Air Fryer Function

Prep time: 10 mins
Cook time: 10 minutes
Serves: 2

Ingredients:

• 2 avocados
• 4 eggs
• 35 g parmesan cheese

Preparation Instructions:

1. Halve the avocado and scoop out the flesh.
2. Crack one egg in each hole of the avocado.
3. Sprinkle the parmesan cheese over the eggs.
4. Place in air fryer basket and cook for 10 minutes at 205°C.

Crunchy 'fried' Chicken

Air fry feature

Prep time: 1 - 12 hours

Cook time: 30 mins

Serves: 3

Ingredients:

- 10 pieces of chicken (mix of wings and drumsticks)
- 240 ml milk
- ½ juice of a lemon
- 50 g breadcrumbs
- 1 tbsp garlic powder
- 1 tbsp lemon pepper

Preparation Instructions:

1. Marinate chicken in milk and lemon juice for up to 12 hours.
2. Mix breadcrumbs, garlic powder and lemon pepper.
3. Coat chicken in the breadcrumb mixture.
4. Airfry for 25 - 30 minutes at 180°C.

Turkey Loaf

Airfryer Function

Prep time: 5 mins

Cook time: 30 mins

Serves: 4

Ingredients:

- 455 g turkey mince
- 100 g breadcrumbs
- 2 tbsp worchester sauce
- 1 tbsp brown sauce
- Seasonings: salt and pepper and garlic powder
- 2 eggs
- 1 tsp onion powder
- 3 tbsp ketchup

Preparation Instructions:

1. In a bowl mix all ingredients together.
2. Line loaf tin with foil.

3. Spoon turkey mixture into the loaf tin.7
4. Put loaf tin in airfryer basket.
5. Cook at 180°C for 30 - 35 minutes until cooked throughout.

Chicken Milanese

Air Fryer Function

Prep time: 10 mins
Cook time: 20 mins
Serves: 3

Ingredients:

- 3 chicken breasts
- 60 g panko breadcrumbs
- 2 tbsp parmesan cheese
- 2 eggs
- Garlic Powder
- Salt and Pepper

Preparation Instructions:

1. Pound 3 chicken fillets using a meat hammer until they are about ½ - 1 cm thick.
2. Season chicken with salt and pepper.
3. Beat 2 eggs.
4. Mix panko breadcrumbs, parmesan cheese, salt and pepper and garlic powder.
5. Prepare your coating station by having the eggs first and then followed by the breadcrumb mix.
6. Dip the chicken into the egg and then the breadcrumbs.
7. Spray chicken with some spray oil.
8. Transfer to the airfryer basket at cook at 200°C for 15 - 20 minutes.

BBQ Chicken Thighs

Airfryer Function

Prep time: 5 mins
Cook time: 25 mins
Serves: 2

Ingredients:

- 4 chicken thighs
- Olive oil
- Salt and Pepper

- 1 tbsp paprika
- 120 g BBQ sauce

Preparation Instructions:

1. Season chicken thighs with olive oil, salt and pepper and paprika
2. Cook in airfryer for 20 minutes at 200°C.
3. After 20 minutes, remove from airfryer and mix with BBQ sauce.
4. Put them back in the airfryer and cook for a further 4 - 5 mins.

Hot Honey Chicken Tenders

Airfryer Function

Prep time: 5 mins
Cook time: 12 mins
Serves: 4

Ingredients:

- 3 chicken breasts
- 80 g crushed crisps (your choice of flavour)
- 1 egg
- Garlic and Onion powder
- 3 tbsp hot sauce
- 3 tbsp honey

Preparation Instructions:

1. Slice chicken breasts into thin slices.
2. Beat egg.
3. Coat the chicken with the beaten egg.
4. Crush crisps and mix with tsp garlic and onion powder.
5. Coat chicken in the crisp mixture.
6. Spray with some spray oil.
7. Cook in airfryer for 12 minutes at 200°C.
8. Once cooked, drizzle 3 tbsp hot sauce and 3 tbsp honey over the chicken.

Chicken Kievs

Airfryer Function

Prep time: 40 mins
Cook time: 25 mins
Serves: 2

Ingredients:

- 2 chicken breasts
- 80 g panko breadcrumbs
- 2 tbsp butter
- 3 x garlic cloves
- 1 tbsp chopped parsley
- Spray Oil
- 1 egg, beaten

Preparation Instructions:

1. In a small bowl, mix butter, minced garlic and parsley together.
2. Wrap the garlic butter tightly in clingfilm and put in freezer for 15 - 20 mins.
3. Butterfly each chicken breast and pound to flatten using a rolling pin.
4. Fill chicken breast with garlic butter, roll in a ball and return to freezer for another 15-20 minutes.
5. Brush chicken with beaten egg and roll in breadcrumbs to coat.
6. Spray each fillet with spray oil.
7. Cook in airfryer at 190°C for 25 minutes.

Turkey Meatballs

Pressure Cook function

Prep time: 10 mins
Cook time: 20 mins
Serves: 4

Ingredients:

- 455 g turkey mince
- 1 small onion, chopped
- 55 g panko breadcrumbs
- 1 tsp dried oregano
- 1 egg
- 1 tsp soy sauce
- 20 g grated parmesan
- 4 x cloves of garlic, minced
- 10 g finely chopped parsley
- Salt and Pepper
- 60 ml milk

Preparation Instructions:

1. In a large bowl, mix together all the ingredients.
2. Use hands to ensure all seasonings have been distributed into the turkey mince.
3. Roll into meatballs. This recipe should make about 15 meatballs.
4. Brown meatballs over a medium heat (about 1 min per side)
5. Add meatballs to the cooking basket and select pressure cooker option.
6. Close the lid and cook for 5 - 6 minutes.
7. Turn off heat and allow a quick release.

8. Ensure meatballs are cooked all the way through before eating.

Strawberry–Glazed Chicken Tenders

Prep Time: 10 minutes
Cook time: 10 minutes
Serves: 4

Ingredients

- 80 g sugar-free strawberry jam
- 3 tablespoons chopped fresh basil, divided
- 1 teaspoon smooth orange juice
- ¼ teaspoon salt
- ¼ teaspoon freshly ground black pepper
- 455 g chicken mini fillets

Preparation Instructions

1. Combine the jam, 2 tablespoons of basil, orange juice, salt, and pepper in a medium bowl; add chicken, then cover the bowl and refrigerate them for 30 minutes up to overnight.
2. Preheat the air fryer at 175 °C for 3 minutes.
3. Add chicken tenderloins to the air fryer basket, and cook them for 4 minute.
4. Flip the chicken tenderloins and cook for an additional 5 minutes until they have an internal temperature of at least 75 °C.
5. Transfer chicken to a large serving plate, and let rest 5 minutes, then garnish with remaining basil and serve warm.

Lemon Pepper Chicken Legs

Grill feature

Prep time: 5 mins
Cook time: 35 mins
Serves: 3 - 4

Ingredients:

- 455 g chicken legs
- 1 tbsp garlic powder
- 1 tbsp lemon pepper
- 1 lemon
- 1 tsp garlic salt
- 1 tsp mixed herbs
- Spray Oil

Preparation Instructions:

1. Place the chicken legs under the Ninja Grill and spray with spray oil.
2. Cut lemon and squeeze the juice directly over the chicken legs as they are cooking.
3. Sprinkle all seasonings over the legs as they cook.
4. Slice the lemon and lay slices on top of the chicken legs as they cook.
5. Press gril and cook for 20 - 25 minutes.
6. Once time is completed, do not open the lid, allow chicken legs to rest for about 10 minutes.

Garlic Turkey Breasts

Sauté feature

Prep time: 1 - 12 hours
Cook time: 30 mins
Serves: 3

Ingredients:

- ½ teaspoon garlic powder
- 4 tablespoons butter
- ¼ teaspoon dried oregano
- 450 g turkey breasts, boneless
- 1 teaspoon pepper
- ½ teaspoon salt
- ¼ teaspoon dried basil

Preparation Instructions:

1. Season turkey on both sides generously with garlic, dried oregano, dried basil, black pepper and salt
2. Select "Sauté" mode on your Ninja Foodi and stir in butter; let the butter melt
3. Add turkey breasts and sauté for 2 minutes on each side
4. Lock the lid and select the "Bake/Roast" setting; bake for 15 minutes at 180°C.

Turkey Meatballs

Pressure Cook function

Prep time: 10 mins
Cook time: 25 mins
Serves: 3

Ingredients:

- 1 teaspoon rapeseed oil
- 60 g chopped carrot

- ¾ teaspoon minced garlic
- 255 g beans, rinsed and drained
- 225 g duck breasts, sliced
- 60 g chopped celery
- 55 g chopped onion
- 120 ml chicken stock
- 180 g diced tomatoes
- Salt and pepper, to taste

Preparation Instructions:

1. Heat oil in Ninja Foodi Pressure Cooker and select "Pressure".
2. Press the "Start/Stop" button and cook duck breasts in it for about 7 minutes.
3. Take out the duck and sauté celery, carrot, onion and garlic in the frying pan for about 7 minutes.
4. Return duck in the pot of Ninja Foodi and stir in stock, beans and tomatoes.
5. Close the pressure Lid and cook for about 10 minutes.
6. Open the pressure Lid and take out

Asian inspired salmon

Airfry Function

Prep time: 5 mins

Cook time: 7 mins

Serves: 2

Ingredients:

- 2 skin on salmon fillets
- 1 tsp white miso paste
- ¼ red chili flakes
- 1 tsp brown sugar
- 1 tsp fish sauce
- 1 tbsp sesame oil
- 1 tbsp rapeseed oil

Preparation Instructions:

1. Mix all ingredients except salmon together to make the marinade.
2. Brush the miso marinade on the salmon fillets.
3. Place the salmon fillets skin side up in the airfryer and cook for 4 minutes at 190°C.
4. Turn fillets so skin is facing down.
5. Return to the airfryer for a further 3 minutes at 190°C.

Spicy Roasted Prawns

Sear / Sauté function

Prep time: 5 mins

Cook time: 5 mins

Serves: 2

Ingredients:

- 200 g prawns
- ¼ tsp salt
- ½ tsp turmeric
- ¼ tsp chili flakes
- 1 tsp cumin
- ½ tsp mustard seeds
- 1 tsp rapeseed oil

Preparation Instructions:

1. Mix all ingredients except prawns and oil in a small bowl.
2. Add oil to spice mix and stir to combine.
3. Toss the prawns in the spice mix.
4. Set Ninja foodi to Medium temperature on Sauté function.
5. Cook for around 5 mins until prawns are cooked throughout.

Creamy Spinach Stuffed Salmon

Airfry Function

Prep time: 10 mins
Cook time: 15 mins
Serves: 2

Ingredients:

- 2 salmon fillets
- 1 tbsp sour cream
- 1 tbsp mayonnaise
- 1 tsp lemon juice
- 20 g fresh spinach
- 2 tsp olive oil
- Salt and Pepper

Preparation Instructions:

1. Cut a pocket across the salmon fillet taking care not to cut the whole way through.
2. Season each salmon fillet with a tsp olive oil and salt and pepper.
3. In a small bowl, mix mayonnaise, sour cream, lemon juice, spinach and pepper.
4. Spoon this mixture into the pocket of the salmon.
5. Airfry at 190°C for 12 - 15 minutes.

Grilled Tuna

Grill Function

Prep time: 5 mins
Cook time: 6 mins
Serves: 2

Ingredients:

- 2 tuna steaks
- Salt and Pepper

Preparation Instructions:

1. Rub salt and pepper into tuna steaks.
2. Press grill and cook each side for 3+ minutes depending on how rare you like your fish.

Scallops with asparagus

Pressure Cooker Function

Prep time: 10 mins

Cook time: 10 mins

Serves: 8

Ingredients:

- 675 g scallops
- 2 tablespoons coconut oil
- 2 teaspoons lemon zest, finely grated
- 40 g shallots, chopped
- 675 g asparagus, chopped
- 2 garlic cloves, minced
- 2 tablespoons fresh lemon juice
- 2 tablespoons fresh rosemary, chopped
- Salt and black pepper

Preparation Instructions:

1. Add oil in Ninja Foodi Pressure Cooker and sauté shallots in it for about 2 minutes.
2. Select "Sear" and press the "Start/Stop" button.
3. Add in garlic and rosemary and Sauté for about 1 minute.
4. Stir in asparagus and lemon zest and cook for about 2 minutes.
5. Add in scallops, lemon juice, salt and pepper and cook for about 5 minutes.

Indian Style Grilled Haddock

Grill Function

Prep time: 30 mins

Cook time: 10 minutes

Serves: 2

Ingredients:

- 2 haddock fillets
- 1 tsp turmeric
- 1tsp paprika
- ¼ tsp red chili powder

- 1 tsp cumin
- 1 ½ tbsp rapeseed oil
- 1 tbsp lemon zest

Preparation Instructions:

1. Marinate the fish for half an hour in the salt, turmeric, paprika, red chili powder, cumin powder, rapeseed oil and lemon zest.
2. Place fish in grill at medium temperature for 5 minutes.
3. Brush any remaining marinade on the fish and lemon zest.
4. Place back under grill until cooked through.

Salt Bake Fish

Air Fryer Function

Prep time: 10 mins
Cook time: 20 minutes
Serves: 3 - 4

Ingredients:

- 260 g fine sea salt
- 1 egg white
- 300 - 400 g slice of salmon
- 1 x clove of garlic, minced
- 1 - 2 parsley sprigs
- 1 tbsp dried rosemary
- 2 slices of lemon

Preparation Instructions:

1. Preheat Ninja Foodi on Bake / Roast setting at 200°C for 5 minutes.
2. Combine sea salt and egg white until they look like wet sand.
3. Put greaseproof paper on the basket with salmon on top.
4. Add garlic, rosemary, parsley and lemon.
5. Finally cover with sea salt and egg mixture.
6. Bake at 200°C for 15 mins until salt turns golden brown.
7. Place on a serving dish and crack opne the salt and brush away the salt.

Miso Cod

Air Fryer Function

Prep time: 4 hours
Cook time: 18 minutes

Serves: 2

Ingredients:

- 2 cod steaks
- 1 tbsp miso paste
- 4 tbsp mirin
- 1 tsp brown sugar

Preparation Instructions:

1. Mix miso paste, mirin and brown sugar and rub it on the cod.
2. Allow to marinate for at least 4 hours.
3. Airfry at 180°C for 9 minutes each side.

Beer-battered Fish

Pressure Cooker Function

Prep time: 10 mins

Cook time: 15 minutes

Serves: 4

Ingredients:

- 450 g codfish cuts
- 125 g flour
- ½ teaspoon baking soda
- 2 tablespoons Cornflour
- 100 ml beer
- 1 beaten egg
- Salt as required
- ¼ teaspoon Cayenne pepper
- 1 tablespoon olive oil
- For Flour Mix
- 85 g of flour
- 1 teaspoon paprika powder
- ½ teaspoon black pepper

Preparation Instructions:

1. Combine flour, cornflour, salt, cayenne pepper, and baking soda in a large bowl. Then add egg and beer, and stir it until it becomes a smooth batter. Let it refrigerate for 20 minutes.
2. Take 85 g flour, paprika, black pepper in a shallow pan.The fish should be at least 2.5 cm thick so that it does not dry out in the Ninja Foodi Pressure Cooker Cook & Crisp Basket.
3. Take a paper towel and pat dry the codfish cuts.Now coat all sides while dipping the fish into the batter.

4. Allow the eggs batter to dip off and again coat it with seasoned flour mix. Any leftover flour can be sprinkled on the fish fillet.
5. Now preheat the Ninja Foodi Pressure Cooker at Air Crisp Mode at 200° C for 5 minutes.
6. Spray both sides of the coated fish fillet with vegetable oil and then place them in the Ninja Foodi Pressure Cooker Cook & Crisp Basket for 12 minutes.

Hake Fillets

Air Fryer Function

Prep time:5 mins
Cook time: 25 mins
Serves: 2

Ingredients:

- 2 hake filelts
- 1 tbsp sesame oil
- 1 lemongrass (white part, cut into 5 slices)
- 5 slices ginger
- 4 cherry tomatoes, halved
- Sauce Ingredients
- 1 tsp fish sauce
- 1 tsp oyster sauce
- 1 tsp lime juice
- 60 ml water

Preparation Instructions:

1. Pour sesame oil on one of the steaming containers.
2. Mix all sauce ingredients in a small bowl.
3. Arrange lemongrass and tomatoes around the hake.
4. Top with ginger.
5. Drizzle sauce over the hake fillets.
6. Pour 720 ml water into the Ninja Foodi pot.
7. Close with pressure lid and cook on high for 13 minutes.
8. Once time is up allow pressure pin to release for 10 minutes.
9. Open lid and remove fish.

Cajun Prawns

Air Crisp Function

Prep time: 5 mins
Cook time: 7 mins

Serves: 4

Ingredients:

- 530 g prawns
- ¼ teaspoon cayenne pepper
- ½ teaspoon old bay seasoning
- ¼ teaspoon smoked paprika
- 1 pinch of salt
- 1 tablespoon olive oil

Preparation Instructions:

1. Preheat Ninja Foodi by pressing the Air Crisp option and setting it to 200°C and timer to 10 minutes
2. Dip the prawns into a spice mixture and oil
3. Transfer the prepared prawns to your Ninja Foodi Grill cooking basket and cook for 5 minutes

Air Crisped Cod with Garlic and Ginger

Air Crisp and Sauté Function

Prep time: 5 mins
Cook time: 15 mins
Serves: 2

Ingredients:

- 2 cod fillets
- 1 tbsp seafood seasoning sauce
- 1-inch ginger, minced
- 2 x cloves of garlic, minced
- 30 ml hot water
- 1 tbsp teriyaki sauce

Preparation Instructions:

1. Rub seafood sauce on the cod, rinse and then pat dry.
2. Place reversible rack in the pot and brush rack and cod fillets with oil.
3. Place cod on the reversible rack.
4. Cook on Air Crisp mode for 10 minutes at 200°C.
5. Remove fish from rack and place on a serving plate.
6. Switch to Sauté mode and add ginger and fry until slightly browned.
7. Add in garlic and fry intil golden brown.
8. Pour in water and teriyaki sauce.
9. Stir for one minute
10. Spoon sauce over the cooked cod fillets.

BBQ ribs

Air Fry Function

Prep time: 5 mins

Cook time: 35 mins

Serves: 3 - 4

Ingredients:

- 1.3 kg pork ribs
- 2 tbsp olive oil
- ½ tsp salt
- ½ tsp pepper
- ½ tsp cayenne pepper
- 1 tsp garlic powder
- 1 tsp paprika
- 240 g BBQ sauce

Preparation Instructions:

1. Mix all spices in a small bowl and add oil to make marinade.
2. Rub marinade into ribs.
3. Wrap ribs in tinfoil and airfry for 30 minutes at 180°C.
4. Remove foil and brush ribs with BBQ sauce.
5. Place back in airfryer for a further 5 minutes.

Beef Bourgignon

Sauté and Pressure Cooker Function

Prep time: 10 mins

Cook time: 45 mins

Serves: 5

Ingredients:

- 900 g stewing beef
- 170 g bacon, chopped
- 1 onion, chopped
- 2 tbsp flour
- 450 ml beef stock
- 1 tsp fresh thyme

- 1 tbsp olive oil
- 1 carrot, chopped
- 6 minced cloves of garlic
- 240 ml red wine
- 2 tbsp tomato paste
- 2 tbsp fresh chopped parsley

- 2 bay leaves
- 450 g mushrooms

Preparation Instructions:

1. Set Ninja Foodi to Sear feature and sauté bacon in 1 tbsp oil until crisp and brown.
2. Remove once cooked.
3. Sear beef until browned using same oil as bacon.
4. Return bacon to the pot and season with salt and pepper.
5. Sprinkle with flour, toss well and cook cook for a further 4 - 5 minutes.
6. Add onions, wine, carrots, stock, tomato paste, garlic and herbs.
7. Stir well.
8. Change to High Pressure function for 30 minutes.
9. After cooking, allow the pressure to release naturally for about 10 minutes.
10. Add chopped mushrooms and carrots and stir to combine.
11. Change function back to Sear.
12. Allow the sauce to thicken for 5 - 10 minutes.
13. Garnish with parsley.

Pulled Pork Burger

Slow Cooker Function

Prep time: 10 mins

Cook time: 4 hours

Serves: 6

Ingredients:

- 240 g BBQ sauce
- 60 ml apple cider vinegar
- 4 minced cloves of garlic

- 120 ml chicken stock
- 1 onion, chopped
- 2 kg pork shoulder

Spice rub mix:
- 55 g dark brown sugar
- 1 tbsp salt
- 2 tsp black pepper
- 1 tsp mustard powder

- 2 tbsp smoked paprika
- 2 tsp chili powder
- 1 tsp ground cumin
- ½ tsp cayenne pepper

Preparation Instructions:

1. In the slow cooker bowl, whisk together BBQ sauce, chicken stock and apple cider vinegar. Add onions and garlic and stir.
2. In a small bowl, combine all the spice mix and rub into the pork.
3. Place the pork in the Ninja Foodi and set to Slow Cooker Mode.
4. Cover and cook on low for 6 hours.

Grilled Lamb Steak

Grill Function

Prep time: 5 mins
Cook time: 12 mins
Serves: 2

Ingredients:

- 2 lamb steaks
- 1 tbsp olive oil
- Salt and Pepper
- 1 tsp oregano
- ½ tsp thyme
- ½ tsp paprika

Preparation Instructions:

1. In a small bowl, combine oil, oregano, thyme, paprika and salt and pepper.
2. Rub this mixture thoroughly into your steaks.
3. Cook on Grill setting for 6 minutes each side (or depending on how rare / well done you enjoy your steak)

Rosemary Lamb Chops

Grill Function

Prep time: 5 mins
Cook time: 12 mins
Serves: 2

Ingredients:

- 700 g lamb chops
- 2 rosemary sprigs
- Salt to taste
- 1 tablespoon olive oil
- 1 tablespoon butter
- ½ tablespoon tomato paste
- 120 ml beef stock
- 1 green onion, sliced

Preparation Instructions:

1. Season the lamb chops with rosemary, black pepper and salt.
2. Pour in the olive oil and stir in the butter to the Ninja Foodi. Set it to sauté.
3. Add the lamb chops and cook for one minute per side. Stir in the rest of the ingredients.

4. Stir well. Cover the pot. Set it to pressure. Cook at high pressure for 5 minutes.

5. Release the pressure naturally.

Beef Ragu

Slow Cooker Function

Prep time: 10 mins

Cook time: 6 hours

Serves: 4 - 6

Ingredients:

- 900 g beef brisket
- Tin of chopped tomatoes
- 5 x garlic cloves, minced
- 300 ml beef stock
- 1 onion, chopped
- 1 tbsp rosemary, basil and oregano
- 2 tbsp tomato puree
- 100 ml red wine
- 1 carrot, chopped
- Salt and Pepper

Preparation Instructions:

1. On Seal function, brown the beef brisket for 3 - 4 minutes.
2. Change to Slow Cook function and add all ingredients.
3. Cook on high for 6 - 7 hours.

Pork Belly

Air Fryer Function

Prep time: 5 mins

Cook time: 15 minutes

Serves: 4 - 6

Ingredients:

- 500 g pork belly
- 2 tsp olive oil
- Salt and Pepper

Preparation Instructions:

1. Preheat on Airfryer Function at 200 °C for 5 minutes.
2. Slice pork belly into 2.5 cm pieces.
3. Rub olive oil into pieces and sprinkle salt and pepper over the pieces too.
4. Arrange pieces in airfryer basket so no pieces are overlapping.
5. Cook for 10 minutes, turning the pieces halfway through.
6. Remove any brown or crispy pieces.

7. Cook for another 3 - 5 minutes to allow thicker pieces to cook.

Lamb Shanks

Pressure Cooker Function

Prep time: 45 mins

Cook time:1 hr 20 mins

Serves: 3 - 4

Ingredients:

- 2 lamb shanks
- 2 garlic cloves, minced
- 1 tbsp brown sugar
- 1 tsp paprika
- 1 tsp cinnamon
- 240 ml red wine
- 30 ml water

- 60 ml olive oil
- 1 onion, chopped
- 1 tsp organo
- 1 bay leaf
- 1 carrot, chopped
- 480 ml stock
- 1 tbsp cornflour

Preparation Instructions:

1. In a bowl, combine lamb, 30 ml oil, brown sugar, oregano, cinnamon, garlic, salt and pepper.
2. Rub mixture onto meat and leave to marinate from 30 minutes to overnight.
3. Using Sauté function, add 30 ml oil and brown the lamb shanks.
4. Remove the lamb and keep it to the side.
5. Add onions, carrots, bay leaf, and remaining marinade. Sauté until onions have softened and become translucent.
6. Pour red wine into the pot and then add back the lamb.
7. Simmer for 10 minutes until cooking liquid has reduced.
8. Add stock and cook for 30 minutes at high pressure.
9. After cooking time allow pressure naturally release.
10. Remove lamb from the pot.
11. Strain the cooking liquid and return it to the pot.
12. In a separate bowl, mix cornflour with water, then add to the pot.
13. Using the Sauté function once again, simmer the sauce until it reaches required consistency.
14. Add lamb back to the pot and allow to sit in the sauce for a few minutes.

Pulled Beef

Saute and Slow Cooker Function

Prep time: 10 mins

Cook time: 4 hours

Serves: 6

Ingredients:

- 1 kg beef joint
- 200 ml bbq sauce
- 4 tbsp soft brown sugar
- 2 tbsp white wine vinegar
- 1 medium onion, chopped
- 1 tbsp Worchestershire sauce
- 2 tbsp American mustard
- 1 tbsp smoked paprika
- 2 tbsp olive oil

Preparation Instructions:

1. Using the Sauté function, sear all sides of the meat until browned.
2. Remove meat from heat.
3. Sauté onion with salt and pepper until onion has softened and is translucent.
4. Add remaining ingredients and 200 ml water and mix well.
5. Change the function to Slow Cooker.
6. Add meat back to the pot and cook for 4 hours on high.
7. After cooking time, remove beef from the pot and shred with 2 forks.

Beef Jerky

Dehydrator Function

Prep time: 5 mins

Cook time: 7 hours

Serves: 4

Ingredients:

- 225 g beef, sliced into ¼ cm-thick strips
- 120 ml of soy sauce
- 2 tablespoons Worcestershire sauce
- 2 teaspoons black pepper
- 1 teaspoon onion powder
- ½ teaspoon garlic powder
- 1 teaspoon salt

Preparation Instructions:

1. Add listed ingredient to a large-sized Ziploc bag, seal it shut.
2. Shake well, seal, and leave it in the fridge overnight.
3. Lay strips on dehydrator trays, making sure not to overlap them.
4. Lock Crisping Lid and set its cooking temperature to 60°C, cook for 7 hours.

Lemon and Garlic Pork Chops

Grill Function

Prep time: 5 mins

Cook time: 15 mins

Serves: 2

Ingredients:

- 2 Pork Chops
- ½ Lemon, juice and zest
- 1 Pinch Pepper
- ½ tbsp Rosemary
- 1 tbsp garlic, minced
- 1 Pinch Salt
- 1 tsp fresh parsley
- 2 tbsp Olive Oil

Preparation Instructions:

1. Combine all ingredients in a large bowl.
2. If possible allow pork to marinate in the bowl for a few hours.
3. Turn the grill setting of your Ninja Foodi on, setting it to pork.
4. Allow the grill to preheat.
5. Once preheated, add the chops.
6. Flip the chops on the demand of the machine.
7. Continue to cook until Ninja Foodi reads 'Get Food'
8. Ensure chops are cooked throughout before eating.

Steak

Air Fry Function

Prep time: 3 mins

Cook time: 10 mins

Serves: 2

Ingredients:

- 450 g sirloin steaks
- Salt and Pepper

Preparation Instructions:

1. Allow steaks to come to room temperature for 10 - 20 minutes before placing in the airfryer basket.
2. Rub salt and pepper into each steak.
3. Set temperature to 180°C and cook for 5 minutes.
4. After the time, turn the steaks and cook for another 5 minutes.
5. Check to see if steak has reached your desired level of doneness.

Indian Style Aubergine

Air Fry Function

Prep time: 5 mins

Cook time: 12 mins

Serves: 3 - 4

Ingredients:

- 2 medium aubergines

Marinade Ingredients:

- 1 tsp red miso paste
- ½ tsp red chili flakes
- 2 tsp rice wine vinegar

- Spray Oil

- 2 tsp sesame oil
- 2 tsp mirin
- 1 tbsp rapeseed oil

Preparation Instructions:

1. Cut stalks from aubergines.
2. Chop each aubergine into 6 - 8 cubes.
3. Combine all marinade ingredients and mix well.
4. Toss the aubergine in the marinade and leave for 30 minutes.
5. Spray the airfryer basket with some spray oil.
6. Preheat the airfryer for 3 minutes at 190°C.
7. Add aubergines and cook for 5 minutes, toss and cook again for a further 5 - 7 minutes.

Mac and Cheese

Pressure and Slow Cooker Function

Prep time: 10 mins

Cook time: 15 mins

Serves: 6 - 8

Ingredients:

- 455 g pasta, macaroni or penne
- 400 g grated cheddar cheese
- 50 g breadcrumbs
- 240 ml low-fat milk
- ½ tsp garlic powder
- ½ tsp onion powder
- Salt and Pepper

Preparation Instructions:

1. Add dry pasta, 960 ml water, garlic and onion powder to the pot.
2. Cook for 4 minutes on High Pressure mode.
3. Use the Venting option to allow pressure to release.
4. Switch to slow cooker setting and add cheese and milk.
5. Stir well until a creamy sauce is formed.
6. Serve topped with breadcrumbs.

Tofu and Pepper Skewers

Grill Function

Prep time: 5 mins
Cook time: 6 mins
Serves: 3 - 4

Ingredients:

- 250 g tofu, cut into small cubes
- 1 red onion, cut into chunks
- 2 tsp red wine vinegar
- ½ tsp oregano
- ½ tsp parsley
- Salt and Pepper

- 1 red pepper, cut into chunks
- Marinade Ingredients:
- 1 tbsp olive oil
- ½ tsp mint

Preparation Instructions:

1. Make skewer marinade by adding all the marinade ingredients together.
2. Add tofu, pepper, and onion to the marinade and mix to ensure it has all been covered with the sauce.
3. Select Grill and time to 6 minutes, allow to preheat.
4. Assemble skewers by alternating between tofu, onion, and pepper. Ensure ingredients have been pushed to near the end of the skewer.
5. Once grill has preheated, put skewers on the grill plate and close lid.
6. After about 3 minutes, open lid to turn the skewers, close the lid, and continue cooking for a further 3 minutes.

Vegetable Curry

Slow Cooker Function

Prep time: 10 mins
Cook time: 6 hours
Serves: 2 - 3

Ingredients:

- 400ml can light coconut milk
- 3 tbsp mild curry paste
- 1 vegetable stock cube
- 1 red chili, deseeded and sliced
- 1 tbsp finely chopped ginger
- 3 garlic cloves, sliced
- 200g butternut squash, cut into chunks
- 1 red pepper, sliced
- 1 small aubergine (about 250g), halved and thickly sliced
- 15g coriander, chopped
- 160g frozen peas, defrosted

Preparation Instructions:

1. Add coconut milk, curry powder, aubergine, butternut squash, chili, ginger, garlic and stock cube into the pot and stir well.
2. Using Slow Cooker setting, cook on low for about 6 hours.
3. Stir in coriander and peas.
4. Allow to warm through and serve!

Spicy Beetroot Burgers

Air Fry Function

Prep time: 5 mins

Cook time: 15 mins

Serves: 3 - 4

Ingredients:

- 1 large fresh beetroot, grated
- 1 onion, chopped finely
- ¼ tsp red chili powder
- 1 tsp curry powder
- 50 g breadcrumbs
- Spray oil
- 3 - 4 crushed garlic cloves
- 1 potato, boiled and cubed
- ½ tsp salt
- ¼ tsp turmeric powder
- Flour and Water paste

Preparation Instructions:

1. Saute the onions and add garlic as the onions begin to turn brown.
2. Add curry powder and cook for 1 - 2 minutes.
3. Add grated beetroot and remaining spices and fry for about 5 minutes.
4. Add the cubed potato and mix well.
5. Season with salt and pepper.

6. Allow mixture to cool.

7. When the mixture has cooled, shape into burgers and dip each burger into the flour and water paste.

8. Airfry at 190°C for 6 minutes and then turn each burger.

9. Cook for a further 2-3 minutes, ensuring the coating has crisped.

Rice and Bean Casserole

Slow Cooker Function

Prep time: 10 mins

Cook time: 6 hours

Serves: 6

Ingredients:

- 1-2 green peppers, diced
- 3 garlic cloves, minced
- 370 g brown rice
- 1 can pinto beans, rinsed and drained
- 1 can black beans, rinsed and drained
- 1 can sweetcorn
- 2 tbsp tomato paste
- ½ tsp ground pepper
- 1 tsp salt
- 1 tsp dried oregano
- 1 tbsp cumin
- 300 ml vegetable stock
- 100 g grated cheddar cheese

Preparation Instructions:

1. Using the Sauté function, brown the onion along with peppers and garlic.

2. Switch to Slow Cooker Function and add all remaining ingredients except cheese.

3. Cook on low for 5 hours.

4. After 5 hours, add cheese and mix well to combine. Cook for another 30 minutes to 1 hour.

Tomato Tortellini Soup

Pressure Cooker Function

Prep time: 5 mins

Cook time: 22 mins

Serves: 4

Ingredients:

- 800 g diced tomatoes
- 480 ml vegetable stock
- 480 ml water
- 2 (500 g) pack cream of tomato soup
- 250 g cream cheese
- 500 g tortellini with ricotta and spinach

Preparation Instructions:

1. Add all ingredients except tortellini and cook under Pressure Cooker High setting for 20 minutes.
2. After 20 minutes, add tortellini and cook for a further 2 minutes.

Curry and Herb Crusted Tofu

Airfryer Function

Prep time: 5 mins

Cook time: 8 minutes

Serves: 2 - 4

Ingredients:

- 1 large egg
- 110 g panko breadcrumbs
- ¼ tsp salt and pepper
- 1 tbsp curry powder
- 2 tsp mixed herbs
- 350 g tofu, sliced and pressed

Preparation Instructions:

1. In a small bowl, mix the curry, mixed herbs, and salt and pepper.
2. Whisk the egg and add about a quarter of the curry mix to the egg.
3. Put the breadcrumbs on a plate.
4. Dip the tofu into the egg and then coat in the breadcrumbs and arrange it in the airfryer basket.
5. Cook at 190°C for 8 minutes, turning the tofu halfway through.

Stuffed Tomatoes

Airfryer Function

Prep time: 12 mins

Cook time: 8 mins

Serves: 2

Ingredients:

- 390 g brown rice, cooked
- 260 g tofu, grilled and chopped
- 4 large red tomatoes
- 4 tbsp basil, chopped
- ¼ tbsp olive oil
- Salt and black pepper
- 2 tbsp lemon juice
- 1 tsp red chili powder
- 50 g Parmesan cheese

Preparation Instructions:

1. Take a large bowl and mix rice, tofu, basil, olive oil, salt, black pepper, lemon juice, and chili powder.
2. Take four large tomatoes and centre core them.
3. Fill the cavity with the rice mixture.
4. Top it off with the cheese sprinkle.
5. Put the tomatoes into the air fryer basket.
6. Set it to Air Fry mode, for 8 minutes at 205°C.

Cauliflower Steaks

Grill Function

Prep time: 5 minutes
Cook time: 15 minutes
Serves: 2

Ingredients:

- 1 head of cauliflower
- Salt and Pepper
- 30 ml olive oil

Preparation Instructions:

1. Cut cauliflower lengthways into steaks of about 2 cm thick.
2. Drizzle olive oil over 'steaks' and season with salt and pepper.
3. Select grill mode and allow the grill to preheat.
4. Cook steaks for 10 minutes before turning.
5. Turn steaks and cook for a further 5 minutes.

Onion Pakodas

Air Fryer Function

Prep time: 10 mins

Cook time: 12 minutes

Serves: 4

Ingredients:

- 2 medium onions, thinly sliced
- 30 g rice flour
- ½ tsp turmeric
- Spray Oil
- 1 tbsp coriander, chopped
- 80 g gram flour
- ½ tsp red chili powder
- 1 tsp carom seeds
- Salt and Pepper
- 2 tsp lemon juice

Preparation Instructions:

1. Rub the onions with a sprinkle of salt and leave to side if possible for 30 minutes.
2. Mix flours, spices and coriander leavers in a bowl.
3. Toss in onions and mix well.
4. Add in few drops of lemon juice.
5. Add some water to make a thick batter.
6. Preheat airfryer to 160°C for about 3 minutes.
7. Spray cup cake cases with spray oil.
8. Add pakoda mixture to each case.
9. Airfry for 6 minutes.
10. Turn over the mixture in the cases and cook for a further 6 minutes.

Cauliflower Hummus

Air Fryer Function

Prep time: 5 mins

Cook time: 6 mins

Serves: 4 - 5

Ingredients:

- 1 head of cauliflower, cut into florets
- 2 tbsp Olive oil
- 1 tsp red chili flakes
- 2 garlic cloves, minced

- 1 (400 g) tin of chickpeas
- 1 tbsp tahini
- Salt and Pepper

Preparation Instructions:

1. Allow cauliflower to marinate in 1 tbsp olive oil, garlic, chili and salt and pepper for 30 minutes.
2. Airfry for 6 minutes at 180°C.
3. Once cooked, blend with chickpeas, tahini and remaining olive oil.

Radishes, Tomato and Burrata

Air Fryer Function

Prep time: 5 mins
Cook time: 8 minutes
Serves: 2

Ingredients:

- 50 g radishes
- 100 g tomatoes
- 100 g burrata
- 1 tbsp Olive oil
- Salt and Pepper

Preparation Instructions:

1. Toss radishes and tomatoes in olive oil and salt and pepper.
2. Line airfryer basket with greaseproof paper.
3. Airfry at 160°C until golden.
4. Chop burrata and toss through the fried radishes and tomatoes.

Kale Stir Fry

Pressure Cooker Function

Prep time: 5 mins
Cook time: 15 minutes
Serves: 4

Ingredients:

- 450 g kale, torn
- 2 tbsp balsamic vinegar
- Salt and black pepper
- 2 leeks, sliced
- 1 tbsp fresh parsley, chopped
- 2 shallots, chopped

• 110 g tomato sauce

Preparation Instructions:

1. In the inner pot, combine the kale with the leeks and the other ingredients.
2. Put the Pressure Lid on, set it to Pressure mode, and cook on high for 15 minutes.
3. Quick-release the pressure for 5 minutes, divide the mix between plates, and serve.

Parmesan Potatoes

Grill / Roast function

Prep time: 10 mins
Cook time: 15 mins
Serves: 8

Ingredients:

• 900 g small rooster potatoes cut into bite-sized chunks
• 2 tbsps olice oil
• 1 tsp dried rosemary
• 1 tsp sea salt
• ½ tsp ground black pepper
• 50 g finely grated Parmesan

Preparation Instructions:

1. Set your Ninja Grill to roast and set the temperature to 200°C.
2. Set the timer for 15 minutes.
3. In a large bowl toss the potato chunks with olive oil, rosemary, salt, and pepper.
4. Arrange in a single layer in the basket.
5. Once the grill has been preheated, cook for 15 to 20 minutes, to the desired doneness.
6. Transfer the potatoes back to the bowl and toss with the parmesan

Grilled Watermelon

Grill Function

Prep time: 5 mins
Cook time: 2 mins
Serves: 6 slices

Ingredients:

• 6 slices of watermelon
• 2 tbsp honey

Preparation Instructions:

1. Select Grill Function on Ninja Foodi and allow to preheat.

2. Brush each slice of watermelon with honey.

3. Place watermelon on grill grate and cook for 2 minutes.

Salsa

Air Fry Function

Prep time: 5 mins

Cook time: 20 mins

Serves: 3 - 4

Ingredients:

- 3 - 4 tomatoes
- 3 - 4 cloves of garlic, minced
- 15 g fresh coriander
- Salt
- ½ medium onion
- 1 - 2 jalapenos
- ½ lime, juiced

Preparation Instructions:

1. Add all ingredients to airfryer except salt, lime juice and coriander.

2. Cook at 200°C for 10 minutes.

3. Toss basket and cook for a further 10 minutes.

4. Add mixture to food processor, including salt, coriander and lime juice.

5. Pulse mixture until it reaches desired consistency.

6. Allow to rest before serving.

Bacon Wrapped Jalapenos

Grill Function

Prep time: 10 mins

Cook time:8 mins

Serves: 3 - 4

Ingredients:

- 12 jalapenos
- 12 slices of bacon
- 200 g cream cheese

Preparation Instructions:

1. Cut jalapenos lengthways and remove seeds if you want to reduce spice level.

2. Scoop cream cheese into one half of the pepper.

3. Place the other side of the jalapeno back together.

4. Wrap pepper with slice of bacon.

5. Preheat on Grill Function.

6. Once preheated, cook for 3 - 4 minutes each side until bacon is fully cooked.

Balsamic Cabbage

Sear and Pressure Function

Prep time: 5 mins

Cook time: 15 mins

Serves: 4

Ingredients:

- 1 green cabbage head, shredded
- Salt and black pepper, to taste
- 2 shallots, chopped
- 1 tbsp sweet paprika
- 2 chicory, trimmed and sliced lengthwise
- 1 tbsp olive oil
- 120 ml chicken stock
- 1 tbsp balsamic vinegar

Preparation Instructions:

1. Set the Foodi to Sear / Sauté mode on medium setting. Add the oil, heat it up, then add the shallots and sauté for 2 minutes.

2. Add the cabbage, chicory, and the other ingredients. Stir to combine.

3. Put the Pressure Lid on. Set to pressure mode and cook on high for 13 minutes.

4. Quick-release the pressure for 5 minutes, then divide the mixture between plates and serve.

Roasted Butternut Squash

Airfryer Function

Prep time: 5 mins

Cook time: 24 mins

Serves: 4

Ingredients:

- 1 medium butternut squash
- 2 tbsp olive oil
- 2 cloves of garlic, minced
- Salt and Pepper

Preparation Instructions:

1. Preheat airfryer for 5 minutes at 200°C.

2. Peel butternut squash and chop into 2.5 cm cubes.

3. Mix butternut squash with oil and garlic until well coated.

4. Season with salt and pepper.

5. Arrange in airfryer in a single layer so no pieces are overlapping.

6. Airfry for 12 minutes, toss basket and cook again for a further 12 minutes.

Baked Potato

Bake Function

Prep time: 5 mins

Cook time: 40 mins

Serves: 2

Ingredients:

- 2 large baking potatoes

Preparation Instructions:

1. Place air crisp basket into the Ninja Foodi Grill.
2. Preheat the Ninja Foodi Grill to 200°C on bake setting.
3. Scrub the potato skin, cleaning any dirt or debris.
4. Using a fork, poke the potato in spots piercing the potato skin at least a ½ cm deep
5. Cook until the potato is cooked throughout.

Pasta Chips

Airfry Function

Prep time: 5 mins

Cook time: 25 minutes

Serves: 4

Ingredients:

- 200 g pasta
- 40 g nutritional yeast
- 1 tsp onion powder
- 1 tbsp lemon juice
- 1 tsp garlic powder
- ½ tsp salt

Preparation Instructions:

1. Cook pasta until al dente.
2. Squeeze lemon juice over pasta and mix well.
3. Add other seasonings and toss to coat.
4. Preheat airfryer for 3 - 5 minutes at 200°C.
5. Arrange pasta in an even layer in airfryer basket and cook for 8 - 12 minutes, shaking the basket 3- 4 times during cooking process.

Lasagne

Slow Cooker Function

Prep time: 25 mins

Cook time: 4 hours

Serves: 4

Ingredients:

- 2 tsp rapeseed oil
- 2 onions, finely chopped
- 4 celery sticks, finely diced
- 4 carrots, finely diced
- 2 garlic cloves, chopped
- 400g lean (5% fat) mince beef
- 400g can chopped tomatoes
- 2 tbsp tomato purée
- 1 tbsp balsamic vinegar
- 1 tbsp fresh thyme leaves
- 6 wholewheat lasagne sheets
- White Sauce
- 400ml whole milk
- 50g wholemeal flour
- 1 bay leaf
- 1 tsp nutmeg
- 15g finely grated parmesan

Preparation Instructions:

1. On Sear / Sauté mode, brown onions, garlic and carrots with some rapeseed oil.
2. Add beef mince and allow to brown.
3. Pour in tomatoes, bouillon, tomato purée, bouillon, balsamic vinegar, thyme and plenty of black pepper.
4. Allow to simmer for about 5 minutes.
5. Remove mixture from pot.
6. In a saucepan add milk, flour, bay leaf and nutmeg. Whisk continuously on heat until cooked.
7. Remove bay leaf and add cheese.
8. Spoon meat mixture into slow cooker and cover with lasagne sheets.
9. Spoon white sauce over the lasagne sheets.
10. Cook for 3 - 4 hours on medium / high heat.

Mexican Chicken with Rice

Pressure Cooker Function

Prep time: 15 mins

Cook time: 10 mins

Serves: 4

Ingredients:

- 450 g chicken breasts boneless
- Salt to taste
- 2-3 minced garlic cloves
- 40 g corn
- 25 g cheese
- 1 tablespoon olive oil
- 185 g uncooked rice
- ½ teaspoon chili flakes
- 255 g black beans
- 120 ml chicken stock
- 2 diced onion

Preparation Instructions:

1. Turn on the Ninja Foodi Deluxe XL Pressure Cooker Mode at 200° C and then add olive oil.
2. Add onions, garlic powder, chicken cubes, chili flakes, and salt once oil is hot and cook it until the protein changes its colour.
3. Dump in black beans and corn alongside chicken stock after turning off the Ninja Foodi Pressure Cooker Pot. Stir well together.
4. Now on top of that, sprinkle uncooked rice and by using the back of the spoon, submerge it into the liquid but don't stir it.
5. Put the lid back on and close the steam valve for nine minutes. After that let it naturally release pressure.
6. Lift the lid, fluff up the rice mixture and add cheese on top, mix it gently and set the top back again for about 3 minutes for the cheese to melt!

Taco Bowls

Airfry Function

Prep time: 5 mins

Cook time: 8 mins

Serves: 2

Ingredients:

- 50 g tomato sauce
- 1 tsp cumin
- ½ tsp cayenne pepper
- 150 g cooked chicken breast
- 2 tortilla bowls (tortilla boats)
- 100 g red pepper, diced
- 1 tsp garlic powder
- Salt and Pepper
- 80 g grated cheese

Preparation Instructions:

1. Mix all ingredients excluding chicken, cheese and tortilla bowls.
2. Spoon chicken mixture into each tortilla boat and sprinkle each boat with half of the cheese.
3. Airfry for 8 mins at 180°C.

Cheesy Beef and Pasta Bake

Pressure Cook function

Prep time: 10 mins
Cook time: 20 mins
Serves: 4

Ingredients:

- 1 onion
- 3 cloves of garlic, minced
- 500 g red pasta sauce
- 300 ml double cream
- 300 g mushrooms
- 600 ml chicken or vegetable stock
- 2 tbsp olive oil
- 2 tsp mixed herbs
- 500 g beef mince
- 500 g pasta
- 75 g mozzarella

Preparation Instructions:

1. On Sauté/Sear mode, brown onion with some olive oil.
2. Once onion is translucent, add mince and cook for 3 mins.
3. Add garlic, pasta sauce, mixed herbs and salt and pepper and cook for a further 2 - 3 mins.
4. Then add double cream, pasta, mushrooms and stock.
5. Change function to pressure cook and cook for 3 mins then quick release.
6. Mix and add some mozzarella cheese and bake at 180°C for another 5 - 10 minutes.

Fish Fingers

Grill Function

Prep time: 15 mins
Cook time: 12 mins
Serves: 8

Ingredients:

- 4 (100 g) fillets of white fish, cut into lengths like fingers
- 120 g plain flour
- 2 large eggs, beaten
- 150 g seasoned breadcrumbs
- 1 tbsp salt

• Spray Oil

Preparation Instructions:

1. Prepare coating station by placing flour in a shallow bowl, eggs in another bowl and breadcrumbs and salt combined in a third bowl.
2. Dredge fish fillets in flour, then in the egg and finally the breadcrumbs.
3. Preheat airfryer at 180°C for 3 - 4 minutes.
4. Grease airfryer basket with spray oil.
5. Arrange fingers in a single layer in airfryer basket.
6. Cook in airfryer for 12 minutes, turning at half way point.

Orange Chicken

Airfryer Function

Prep time: 10 mins
Cook time: 20 mins
Serves: 4

Ingredients:

- 455 g chicken breasts, diced into cubes
- 2 tbsp cornflour
- Orange Sauce
- 120 ml orange juice
- 2 tbsp brown sugar
- 1 tbsp soy sauce
- 1 tbsp rice wine vinegar
- ¼ tsp ground ginger
- Zest of one orange
- 2 tsp cornflour (mixed with 2 tsp water)

Preparation Instructions:

1. Preheat airfryer to 200°C.
2. Mix diced chicken and cornflour in a bowl until chicken is completel covered.
3. Airfry chicken for 8 minutes, shaking the basket halfway through.
4. Combine orange juice, brown sugar, rice wine vinegar, soy sauce, ginger and orange zest in a saucepan over a medium heat.
5. Bring to a simmer and cook for 5 minutes.
6. Add cornflour slurry to the sauce and simmer for one minute.
7. Remove chicken from the airfryer and add to the sauce.
8. Serve with rice!

Pork Meatballs

Airfryer Function

Prep time: 15 mins
Cook time: 16 mins
Serves: 4

Ingredients:

- 455 g pork mince
- 1 large egg
- 1 tbsp gochujang
- 1 tsp tamari
- ¼ tsp ground ginger
- 30 g plain gluten-free bread crumbs
- 1 spring onion, whites minced, greens sliced, divided
- 4 tbsp orange marmalade

Preparation Instructions:

1. Preheat air fryer at 175 °C for 3 minutes.
2. Lightly grease the air fryer basket with cooking oil.
3. Combine pork, egg, gochujang, tamari, ginger, bread crumbs, and minced spring onion whites in a large bowl. Form the mixture into sixteen meatballs.
4. Add eight meatballs to air fryer basket and cook them for 6 minutes
5. Flip meatballs. Cook an additional 2 minutes. Transfer to a large plate. Do the same with the remaining meatballs.
6. Garnish the meatballs with sliced spring onion greens and marmalade, and then serve warm.

Sausage and Butterbean Casserole

Slowcooker Function

Prep time: 20 mins
Cook time: 3 hrs 15 mins
Serves: 6

Ingredients:

- 2 tbsp olive oil
- 454g pack Cumberland sausages
- 2 red onions, cut into wedges
- 2 celery sticks, trimmed and sliced
- 1 garlic clove, sliced
- 150g mushrooms, quartered

- 150g arrots
- 1 leek, trimmed and sliced
- ½ tsp crushed chillies
- 2 x 400g tins butter beans, drained and rinsed
- 400g tin chopped tomatoes
- 300ml red wine
- 1 chicken stock cube, made up to 800ml
- 10g fresh rosemary, leaves only
- 4 tbsp cornflour, mixed with 5 tbsp water

Preparation Instructions:

1. Heat the oil in Sear / Sauté mode and fry the sausages for 6-7 mins, turning frequently, until golden.
2. Add the onions, celery, garlic and mushrooms to the pot and cook in the remaining oil for 4-5 mins, stirring occasionally, until beginning to soften.
3. Add the carrots and leek.
4. Mix the remaining ingredients together in a bowl, then add to the pot and season well.
5. Cook on high for 3 hrs or until thick and bubbling.

BBQ Chicken Loaded Sweet Potatoes

Airfry Function

Prep time: 5 mins
Cook time: 45 mins
Serves: 4

Ingredients:

- 6 large sweet potatoes
- 600 g boneless chicken thighs
- 160 g bbq sauce

Preparation Instructions:

1. Preheat airfryer to 220°C for 5 minutes.
2. Scrub the sweet potatoes and pierce holes about 1 cm deep through the skin.
3. Cook in airfryer for 25 minutes or until softened.
4. Once potatoes are cooked, remove from airfryer basket and put chicken thighs in the basket and cook for 20 minutes.
5. When chicken is cooked all the way through, remove and shred with two forks.
6. Mix bbq sauce throughout the chicken.
7. Halve the potatoes and scoop out the flesh and mix with chicken.
8. Spoon chicken mixture back into sweet potato skins and put back into sweet potato for 5 mins.

Chicken Wings

Airfryer Function

Prep time: 10 mins

Cook time: 45 mins

Serves: 4

Ingredients:

- 900 g chicken wings
- Salt
- Freshly ground black pepper
- Spray Oil
- 60 g hot sauce (such as Frank's)
- 4 tablespoons melted butter
- 1 teaspoon Worcestershire sauce
- ½ teaspoon garlic powder

Preparation Instructions:

1. Season the wings with salt and pepper. Spray the inside of the airfryer basket with spray oil.
2. Put the chicken wings in the airfryer basket.
3. Set temperature to 205°C, and set time to 45 minutes.
4. When the time reaches 22 minutes, press START/STOP to pause the cooking. Remove the basket and flip the chicken. Put basket back into airfryer
5. When cooking is complete, remove the chicken wings.
6. Meanwhile, combine the hot sauce, butter, Worcestershire sauce, and garlic powder in a large bowl.
7. Add the cooked wings to the mixture and toss gently to coat.

Penne Pasta with Ham

Pressure Cook function

Prep time: 15 mins

Cook time: 8 mins

Serves: 4

Ingredients:

- 1 Tbsp olive oil
- 80 g diced onions
- 3 cloves minced garlic
- 350 g cubed fully cooked ham
- ½ tsp dried parsley

- ½ tsp dried basil
- ¼ tsp dried oregano
- ¼ tsp pepper
- ¼ tsp red pepper flakes
- 720 ml chicken stock
- 480 ml low fat milk
- 30 g. flour
- 400 g penne noodles, uncooked
- 200 g frozen peas thawed
- 50 g Parmesan cheese

Preparation Instructions:

1. Place 1 Tbsp olive oil in bottom of pot. Turn on Pressure Cooker Function.
2. Saute ham and onions until onions are translucent. Add garlic, parsley, basil, oregano, pepper and red pepper flakes; cook for 1-2 minutes.
3. Stir in stock, milk, and flour. Whisk until combined. Add the rest of the ingredients except Parmesan cheese.
4. Set to high pressure for 8 minutes.
5. After it is done, let the pressure naturally release for about five minutes, and then change to quick release until all the pressure is gone.
6. Sprinkle Parmesan cheese on top of pasta.

Turkey Chili

Pressure Cooker Function

Prep time: 10 mins
Cook time: 25 mins
Serves: 4

Ingredients:

- 2 tablespoons olive oil
- 455 g turkey mince
- 1 medium onion, finely diced
- 1 medium green pepper, cored and finely diced
- 3 medium carrots, peeled and thinly sliced
- 3 stalks celery, thinly sliced
- 3 cloves garlic, minced
- 1 (700 g) can crushed tomatoes
- 1 (375 g) can black beans, drained and rinsed
- 1 (120 g) can chopped green chiles, drained
- 120 ml water

- 3 tablespoons chili powder
- 1 ½ teaspoons ground cumin
- 1 teaspoon salt

Preparation Instructions:

1. Turn the sauté setting on and heat the oil until shimmering. Add the turkey and cook, stirring constantly to break up the meat into small pieces, until no longer pink, about 4 minutes.
2. Add the onion, pepper, carrots, celery, and garlic.
3. Cook, stirring occasionally, for 3 minutes.
4. Add the tomatoes, black beans, green chiles, water, chili powder, cumin, salt. Stir to combine.
5. Secure the lid and close the vent. Set the cook time for 20 minutes at high pressure.
6. When the cook time is complete, quick release the pressure.
7. Stir the chili. Taste and season with salt, soy sauce or tamari, and other seasonings as needed. Serve the chili with your desired toppings.

Pineapple Chicken

Pressure Cooker Function

Prep time: 2 hours

Cook time:10 mins

Serves: 2

Ingredients:

- 2 chicken breasts, chopped into small cubes
- 1 tbsp onion paste
- 4 tbsp teriyaki sauce
- 2 tbsp pineapple juice
- 1 tbsp ginger garlic paste
- Salt and pepper to taste
- Fresh coriander to garnish

Preparation Instructions:

1. Take a large bowl and combine all ingredients. Refrigerate it overnight.
2. Now remove it from the refrigerator and place the leftover marination in the bowl.
3. Place the chicken steak directly in the Ninja Foodi Pressure Cooker Pot.
4. Now over Ninja Foodi Pressure Cooker High Pressure Cook setting, cook the chicken for 3 minutes and use the reserved marinade to baste when meat is cooked halfway.
5. Now turn over the meat for five to seven minutes to cook and do this until the meat is cooked properly.
6. Turn off and plate the chicken, and garnish it with fresh coriander.

Parmesan Goujans

Airfry Function

Prep time: 5 mins

Cook time:12 mins

Serves: 4

Ingredients:

- 300 g chicken breast, sliced
- 20 g cornflakes, crushed
- 2 tsp mixed herbs
- Spray Oil
- 1 egg, beaten
- 5 g parmesan
- 1 tsp garlic powder

Preparation Instructions:

1. Mix cornflakes, parmesan, mixed herbs and garlic powder together in a small bowl.
2. Dip each chicken piece in beaten egg followed by cornflake mix.
3. Spray each goujan with spray oil.
4. Cook in airfryer at 180°C for 12 minutes or until coating is golden and crisp and chicken is cooked through.

Slowcooker Roast Chicken

Slow Cooker Function

Prep time: 5 mins

Cook time: 5 hours

Serves: 5 -6

Ingredients:

- 1 whole chicken
- 2 - 3 potatoes, chopped
- Fresh rosemary and thyme
- 150 ml chicken stock
- 2 carrots, chopped
- 4 garlic cloves
- 1 tbsp Olive Oil
- Salt and Pepper

Preparation Instructions:

1. Add potatoes and vegetables to pot and lay chicken on top.
2. Add remaining ingredients and cook on high for 5 hours.

Dulche de Leche Banana Muffins

Air Fry Function

Prep time: 5 mins

Cook time: 12 mins

Serves: 6

Ingredients:

- 2 bananas
- 60 g plain flour
- 1 tbsp chocolate chips
- 2 tbsp coconut flakes
- 1 egg
- 3 tbsp dulce de leche

Preparation Instructions:

1. Mix bananas, egg, flour, chocolate chips and shredded coconut.
2. Line a muffin tin with muffin cases.
3. Add 1 tbsp of mix to each muffin case, then spoon 1 tsp of dulce de leche followed by ½ tbsp more of muffin mix.
4. Airfry for 12 minutes at 160°C

Crunchie Fudge Slow Cooker

Slow Cooker Function

Prep time: 5 mins

Cook time: 45 mins

Serves: 8 - 12

Ingredients:

- 400 g cadbury chocolate
- 1 tin of condensed milk
- 1 tsp vanilla extract
- 15 g butter
- 4 x crunchie chocolate bars

Preparation Instructions:

1. Put the chocolate, butter, condensed milk and vanilla extract in the slow cooker and cook on

high for 45 mins, stirring every 15 minutes.
2. After 45 minutes, chop the crunchie bars and stir into the mix.
3. Line a tin with greaseproof paper and pour the mixture in.
4. Set in the fridge for 5 hours before chopping into pieces.

Chocolate Chip Cookies

Air Crisp and Pressure Cooker Function

Prep time: 5 mins
Cook time: 10 mins
Serves: 8

Ingredients:
- 115 g butter
- 55 g sugar
- 1 egg
- 1 teaspoon vanilla essence
- 30 g light brown sugar
- ½ teaspoon baking soda
- ¼ teaspoon salt
- 85 g plain flour
- 170 g chocolate chips

Preparation Instructions:
1. Preheat the Ninja Foodi Pressure Cooker at Air Crisp Mode at 200° C then grease a metal cookie pan that fits the Ninja Foodi Pressure Cooker. You can use the cookie cutter and place it in a baking tray.
2. Combine butter, brown sugar, and sugar, and cream.
3. Now add vanilla essence and egg. Mix it well until combined.
4. Add in baking soda, flour, and salt. Now stir in chocolate chips. Give it a good mix.
5. Flatten the cookie dough and press it in the bottom of the greased pan. Dump it in the Ninja Foodi Pressure Cooker and bake for ten to 12 minutes until it becomes slightly brown around the edges!

Grilled Pineapple

Airfryer Function

Prep time: 5 mins
Cook time: 10 mins
Serves: 4

Ingredients:

- 1 whole Pineapple, peeled and cut into slices
- 4 tbsp unsalted butter, melted
- 55 g brown sugar
- 50 g sugar
- 2 tsp vanilla
- 1 tsp cinnamon

Preparation Instructions:

1. Place the cut pineapple into a large bowl.
2. Pour the melted butter into the bowl, and toss the pineapple until all of the pieces are well coated with the butter.
3. Add in the sugars, cinnamon, and vanilla. Toss the pineapple until they are evenly coated in the mixture.
4. Place the coated pineapple slices into the air fryer basket.
5. Cook at 160°C for about 10 minutes.
6. Halfway through cooking, toss the pineapple and pour any remaining butter and sugar mixture from the bowl onto the pineapple.

Apple, Blueberry and Cinnamon Oatloaf

Airfryer Function

Prep time: 5 mins
Cook time: 30 mins
Serves: 5

Ingredients:

- 120 g oats
- 2 eggs
- 200 g natural yogurt
- 1 ripe banana
- 80 g grated apple
- 60 g blueberries
- 1 tbsp sweetener
- 1 tbsp cinnamon

Preparation Instructions:

1. Mix all ingredients in a bowl.
2. Line a loaf tin with greaseproof paper.
3. Spoon mixture into loaf tin and put loaf tin in airfryer basket
4. Cook for about 30 minutes at 180°C.

Lemon Cheesecake

Slow Cooker Function

Prep time: 14 mins

Cook time: 4 hours

Serves: 10 -12

Ingredients:

For Crust:

- 135 g almond flour
- 3 tablespoons sugar-free peanut butter
- 1 large egg, beaten
- 4 tablespoons butter, melted
- 3 tablespoons Sweetener

For Filling:

- 250 g ricotta cheese
- 30 g Sweetener
- 70 g heavy cream
- 3 large egg yolks
- 1 tablespoon vanilla extract
- 600 g cream cheese, softened
- 2 teaspoons liquid stevia
- 2 large eggs
- 1 tablespoon fresh lemon juice

Preparation Instructions:

1. Grease the Ninja Foodi's insert.
2. For crust: add all the ingredients and mix until well combined.
3. In the pot of prepared of Ninja Foodi, place the crust mixture and press to smooth the top surface.
4. With a fork, prick the crust at many places.
5. For filling: in a food processor, stir in the ricotta cheese and pulse until smooth.
6. In a large bowl, add the ricotta, cream cheese, sweetener and stevia and with an electric mixer, beat over medium speed until smooth.
7. In another bowl, stir in the heavy cream, eggs, egg yolks, lemon juice and vanilla extract and beat until well combined.
8. Stir in the egg mixture into cream cheese mixture and beat over medium speed until just combined.
9. Place the prepared filling mixture over the crust evenly.
10. Close the Ninja Foodi's lid with a pressure lid and select "Slow Cook".
11. Set on "Low" for 3-4 hours.
13. Place the pan onto a wire rack to cool.
14. Refrigerate to chill for at least 6-8 hours before serving.

Carrot Cake

Bake Function

Prep time: 10 mins

Cook time: 40 mins

Serves: 12

Ingredients:

- 150 g sugar
- 2 ½ tbsp Hot Water
- 1 tsp baking soda
- 1 tsp cinnamon
- ¼ tsp nutmeg
- 2 carrots, grated

- 240 ml Oil
- 3 eggs
- 180 g plain flour
- 1 tsp baking powder
- Pinch of Salt
- 80 g walnuts

FROSTING

- 115 g unsalted butter, softened
- 1 tsp vanilla
- 40 g chopped walnuts to garnish

- 200 g cream cheese, softened
- 350 g Icing sugar

Preparation Instructions:

1. Mix together the sugar, oil, hot water, eggs, and baking soda.
2. Add in the flour, cinnamon, baking powder, nutmeg, and salt.
3. Fold in the carrots and walnuts.
4. Coat baking pan with spray oil and evenly spread in the batter.
5. Place the pan on the wire trivet in the lowest position and sit inside the pot of the Ninja Foodi.
6. Turn the Ninja Foodi Multi-Cooker to bake and then bake at 160°C for 40 minutes or until when poked with a toothpick in the deepest part it comes out clean.
7. Carefully remove from the foodi and place on a wire rack to cool.
8. While the cake is cooking whisk together the butter, cream cheese, vanilla and icing sugar to make the frosting. If it's too runny, add additional icing sugar in small increments or place the frosting in the fridge to harden.
9. Once the cake is fully cooled, carefully release it by using a spatula and releasing the sides, flip it onto the plate you will be using to serve it on.
10. Once it's ready, frost with the frosting and garnish with additional walnuts.

Mini Tarts

Bake Function

Prep time: 45 mins

Cook time: 20 mins

Serves: 12

Ingredients:

Base:

- 50 g unsalted butter
- 1 egg yolk

- 100 g flour
- 30 g sugar

- Salt

Toppings:
- Fruits of choice

Preparation Instructions:

1. Mix all ingredients well until a dough like consistency.
2. Cover with foil and leave in freezer for 45 minutes.
3. Remove from foil, roll and cut to desired shape.
4. Using Bake Function, cook for 20 mins at 180°C.
5. Chop chosen fruit and arrange on the top of the cooked tarts.

Cream Egg Croissant Balls

Airfryer Function

Prep time: 5 mins
Cook time:8 mins
Serves: 4

Ingredients:
- 1 tube of croissant dough
- 4 cream eggs

Preparation Instructions:

1. Unroll croissant dough on flat surface.
2. Wrap each cream egg with the croissant dough.
3. Airfry at 170°C for 8 minutes.

Peanut Butter Balls

Dehydrator Function

Prep time: 5 mins
Cook time: 4 hours
Serves: 8 - 10

Ingredients:
- 185 g coconut, shredded
- 560 g dried chopped Apples
- 170 g Peanut Butter
- 1 ½ tsp Vanilla extract

Preparation Instructions:

1. Mix all ingredients together.
2. Mold into small balls using your hands.

3. Put Foodi on Dehydrator mode and place balls in the dehydrator for 4 hours until balls are crispy on the outside

Strawberry Thumprint Cookies

Airfryer Function

Prep time: 10 mins

Cook time: 8 mins

Serves: 16 cookies

Ingredients:

- 6 Tablespoons Butter
- 45 g icing sugar
- 80 g plain flour
- 80 g strawberry jam

Preparation Instructions:

1. Cream the butter and sugar.
2. Add flour and mix, use your hands to bring the dough together.
3. Wrap dough in cling film and leave to rest for 10 minutes
4. Divide dough into 16 equal parts.
5. Roll each part into a ball and make an indent on the top of each ball with your thumb.
6. Spoon jam into the indentation.
7. Airfry at 170°C for 8 - 10 minutes.
8. Allow to cool completely before eating.

Tapioca Pudding

Slow Cooker Function

Prep time: 5 mins

Cook time: 4 hours

Serves: 4

Ingredients:

- 960 ml milk
- 75 g tapioca pearls
- 1 tsp vanilla essence
- 100 g sugar
- 1 egg, lightly beaten
- ¼ tsp salt

Preparation Instructions:

1. Mix all ingredients together.
2. Cook for 4 hours on Slow Cooker mode, stirring every 30 minutes if possible.

Beef and Sweet Potato Stew

Pressure Cooker Function

Prep time: 10 mins

Cook time: 10 mins

Serves: 4

Ingredients:

- 455 g lean beef mince
- 1 onion, chopped
- 2 carrots, chopped
- 1 tbsp garlic granules
- 2 garlic cloves, minced
- 2 sweet potatoes, diced into cubes
- 2 peppers, chopped
- 2 tbsp mixed herbs
- 1 tsp salt
- 240 ml beef stock

Preparation Instructions:

1. Place all ingredients into Ninja Foodi pot.
2. Pressure Cook on high for 15 minutes, then quick release.

Beef and Corn Stew

Pressure Cooker Function

Prep time: 10 mins

Cook time: 30 mins

Serves: 4 - 6

Ingredients:

- 240 ml beef stock
- 4 medium potatoes, diced
- 1 onion, chopped
- 675 g beef tenderloin
- 2 tbsp garlic, minced
- 4 tbsp Worchestershire sauce
- 1 tsp thyme
- 1 tsp rosemary
- 1 can of chickpeas
- 1 can of sweetcorn
- 1 jar of sliced carrots

Preparation Instructions:

1. Add all ingredients to the pot except chickpeas, sweetcorn and carrots.
2. Turn Ninja Foodi to pressure cooker mode and cook on high for 25 minutes, followed by quick release.
3. Add chickpeas, sweetcorn and carrots to the pot and stir.
4. Allow stew to rest for 5 minutes before serving.

Toscana Soup

Sear / Sauté Function

Prep time: 10 mins
Cook time: 25 mins
Serves: 4 - 6

Ingredients:

- 455 g sausage
- 450 g diced potatoes
- 115 g butter
- 1 tsp oregano
- 1.2 L milk
- 480 ml chicken stock
- 1 onion, chopped
- 50 g kale, chopped

Preparation Instructions:

1. Turn Ninja Foodi to Sear/Sauté mode.
2. Crumble sausage into the pot and brown for about 10 minutes.
3. Drain the grease and discard.
4. Stir in the milk, potatoes, chicken stock, butter, onion and oregano.
5. Bring to a boil and reduce heat to medium.
6. Simmer until potatoes are tender.
7. Stir in kale and cook for a further 10 minutes.

Lamb and Carrot Stew

Slow Cooker Function

Prep time: 10 mins
Cook time: 9 hours Serves: 3

Ingredients:

- 340 g lamb chops, trimmed
- 120 ml vegetable stock
- 2½ carrots, chopped
- 1 onion, chopped
- Salt and black pepper

Preparation Instructions:

1. Add all the ingredients in Ninja Foodi and mix well. Select "Slow Cook".
2. Cover the pressure Lid and press the start button
3. Cook for about 9 hours on low.

Chicken Noodle Soup

Slow Cooker Function

Prep time: 10 mins
Cook time: 25 mins
Serves: 6

Ingredients:

- 1 medium onion, chopped
- 200 g carrots, ½ cm slices
- 1.4 L chicken stock
- ½ tsp pepper
- ½ tsp. dried marjoram
- ½ tsp. sage
- 455 g raw chicken, cubed
- 240 g celery, ½ cm slices
- 2 cloves garlic, minced
- 1 tsp. salt
- ½ tsp. dried thyme
- ½ tsp. dried rosemary
- 2 bay leaves
- 150 g egg noodles

Preparation Instructions:

1. Add all ingredients to pot excep chicken and noodles.
2. Stir to ensure all seasonings have been mixed well throughout the soup.
3. Add the chicken and noodles to the pot.
4. Select Pressure Cooker mode and cook on this setting for 3 minutes.
5. Allow pressure to naturally release for 5 minutes.
6. Remove bay leaves before serving.

Chicken Bean Chili

Pressure Cooker and Sear/Sauté Function

Prep time: 10 mins
Cook time: 25 mins
Serves: 4 - 6

Ingredients:

- 455 g chicken breast
- 1 tbsp olive oil
- 1 onion, diced

- 1 pepper, diced
- 800 ml chicken stock
- 375 g cannellini beans, drained and rinsed
- 1 tsp. cumin
- 1 tbsp. fresh cilantro, chopped
- ½ tsp. smoky paprika
- 1 tsp. garlic powder
- 1 tsp. onion powder
- 1 tbsp. lime juice

Preparation Instructions:
1. Add chicken and 240 ml water to Ninja Foodi.
2. Set to Pressure Cook mode and cook for 10 minutes.
3. Once cooked, remove chicken and discard cooking liquid.
4. Change setting to Sear/Sauté and heat oil.
5. Saute onions and any other vegetables.
6. Shred the cooked chicken with two forks.
7. Add chicken back to pot and remaining ingredients.
8. Bring to boil and simmer for 10 minutes.

Corn Chowder with Potatoes

Sear / Sauté and Pressure Cooker Function

Prep time: 15 mins

Cook time:20 mins

Serves: 8

Ingredients:
- 455 g bacon, cut into 1 cm strips
- 2 medium stalks celery, diced
- 1 medium yellow onion, peeled and chopped
- 1 medium carrot, diced
- 2 cloves garlic, minced
- 960 ml vegetable stock
- 675 g baby yellow potatoes, quartered
- 1 (375 g) can corn
- 1 (370 g) can creamed corn
- 2 teaspoons salt
- ¼ teaspoon black pepper
- ¼ teaspoon cayenne pepper
- 240 ml whole milk

• 4 medium green onions, sliced

Preparation Instructions:

1. Put Ninja Foodi to Sear/Sauté mode.
2. Add bacon and cook for 5 - 8 minutes.
3. Remove from pot and place on paper towels.
4. Add celery, onions and carrots and cook for 5 minutes.
5. Add garlic and cook for a further 2 -3 minutes.
6. Pour in stock and deglaze the pot.
7. Mix in corn, creamed corn, salt, black pepper, and cayenne.
8. Change setting to Pressure Cooker.
9. Cook on high for 3 minutes.
10. Allow pressure to release naturally.
11. Whisk in milk before serving.

Pea and Ham Soup

Slow Cooker Function

Prep time: 5 mins

Cook time: 3 hours

Serves: 6 - 8

Ingredients:

• 450 g cooked ham
• 1 onion, chopped
• 1 ½ L vegetable stock
• 2 bay leaves
• 700 g frozen peas

Preparation Instructions:

1. On Slow Cooker mode, cook onion, ham, bay leaves and stock on high for 2 hours.
2. Remove the ham and add the peas and cook for a further 30 mins - 1 hour.
3. Shred the ham with two forks.
4. Remove bay leaves from mixture.
5. Add ham back to pot.
6. Blitz with a hand blender to reach desired consistency.

Carrot and Coriander Soup

Sear/ Sauté and Slow Cooker Function

Prep time: 5 mins

Cook time: 4 hours

Serves: 6

Ingredients:

- 2 tsp cumin seeds
- Pinch chilli flakes
- 2 tbsp olive oil
- 600g carrots, washed and coarsely grated
- 140g split red lentils
- 1L vegetable stock
- 125ml milk

Preparation Instructions:

1. On Sear/Sauté mode, fry cumin seeds and chili flakes.
2. Add remaining ingredients and change to Slow Cooker Function.
3. Cook on high for 4 hours.

Tortilla Soup

Sear/ Sauté and Slow Cooker Function

Prep time: 5 mins

Cook time: 4 hours

Serves: 5

Ingredients:

- 1 tbsp extra virgin olive oil
- 1 tbsp. garlic
- 110 g white onion, diced
- 2 tsp chili powder
- 2 tsp cumin
- 960 ml chicken stock
- 1 (700 g) can fire-roasted tomatoes
- 4 tbsp tomato paste
- 3-4 chipotle peppers in adobo, chopped and sauce from the can
- 454 g bag raw cauliflower rice
- Juice from 1 lime
- Pinch of sea salt
- 675 g chicken breast, raw
- Fresh corinader

Preparation Instructions:

1. Set the pot to the Saute function on low. Once it heats up, add the oil, garlic and onions. Saute

for 2 – 3 minutes.
2. Add in the chili powder and cumin.
3. Add the remaining ingredients and stir well.
4. Change to Slow Cooker Function and cook on high for 4 -6 hours.
5. Remove chicken and shred with forks.
6. Return chicken to pot and mix very well.
7. Season with salt and pepper before serving.

Prawn Chowder

Sear/ Sauté and Slow Cooker Function

Prep time: 5 mins

Cook time: 4 hours

Serves: 8 - 10

Ingredients:

- 80 g chopped onion
- 2 tsp butter
- 2 cans (300 g) evaporated milk
- 2 cans condensed cream of potato soup, undiluted
- 2 cans condensed cream of chicken soup, undiluted
- 1 can (175 g) sweetcorn, drained
- 1 tsp cajun seasoning
- ½ tsp garlic powder
- 900 g peeled and deveined cooked small prawns
- 75 g cream cheese, cubed

Preparation Instructions:

1. Saute onion in butter on the Sear/Saute setting of the Ninja Foodi.
2. Add all ingredients except prawns and cream cheese to the pot and change to slow cooker setting
3. Cook on low for 3 hours.
4. Add prawns and cream cheese and cook for a further 30 minutes.

Tomato Soup with Basil

Sear/ Sauté and Pressure Cooker Function

Prep time: 5 mins

Cook time: 10 mins

Serves: 4

Ingredients:

- 2 tbsp olive oil
- 1 medium yellow onion, peeled and chopped
- 2 cloves garlic, minced
- 4 (360 g) cans diced tomatoes
- 480 ml vegetable stock
- 10 g fresh basil, chopped
- 2 tablespoons sugar
- 1 teaspoon salt
- 240 g heavy whipping cream

Preparation Instructions:

1. Put oil and onion into cooking pot and choose Sear / Sauté Mode.
2. Cook onion for 2 minutes until soft.
3. Add in garlic and cook 30 seconds. Turn off.
4. Add tomatoes, vegetable stock, basil, sugar, and salt to pot and stir to combine.
5. Change setting to Pressure Cooker.
6. Set Quick Release and time to 7 minutes.
7. When cooking is complete, let pressure release quickly by turning it into vent position.
8. Blend soup with an immersion blender.
9. Once blended, whisk in heavy whipping cream and serve.

MEASUREMENT CONVERSION CHART

VOLUME EQUIVALENTS(DRY)

US STANDARD	METRIC (APPROXIMATE)
1/8 teaspoon	0.5 mL
1/4 teaspoon	1 mL
1/2 teaspoon	2 mL
3/4 teaspoon	4 mL
1 teaspoon	5 mL
1 tablespoon	15 mL
1/4 cup	59 mL
1/2 cup	118 mL
3/4 cup	177 mL
1 cup	235 mL
2 cups	475 mL
3 cups	700 mL
4 cups	1 L

VOLUME EQUIVALENTS(LIQUID)

US STANDARD	US STANDARD (OUNCES)	METRIC (APPROXIMATE)
2 tablespoons	1 fl.oz.	30 mL
1/4 cup	2 fl.oz.	60 mL
1/2 cup	4 fl.oz.	120 mL
1 cup	8 fl.oz.	240 mL
1 1/2 cup	12 fl.oz.	355 mL
2 cups or 1 pint	16 fl.oz.	475 mL
4 cups or 1 quart	32 fl.oz.	1 L
1 gallon	128 fl.oz.	4 L

TEMPERATURES EQUIVALENTS

FAHRENHEIT(F)	CELSIUS(C) (APPROXIMATE)
225 °F	107 °C
250 °F	120 °C
275 °F	135 °C
300 °F	150 °C
325 °F	160 °C
350 °F	180 °C
375 °F	190 °C
400 °F	205 °C
425 °F	220 °C
450 °F	235 °C
475 °F	245 °C
500 °F	260 °C

WEIGHT EQUIVALENTS

US STANDARD	METRIC (APPROXIMATE)
1 ounce	28 g
2 ounces	57 g
5 ounces	142 g
10 ounces	284 g
15 ounces	425 g
16 ounces (1 pound)	455 g
1.5 pounds	680 g
2 pounds	907 g

The Dirty Dozen and Clean Fifteen

The Environmental Working Group (EWG) is a nonprofit, nonpartisan organization dedicated to protecting human health and the environment Its mission is to empower people to live healthier lives in a healthier environment. This organization publishes an annual list of the twelve kinds of produce, in sequence, that have the highest amount of pesticide residue-the Dirty Dozen-as well as a list of the fifteen kinds ofproduce that have the least amount of pesticide residue-the Clean Fifteen.

THE DIRTY DOZEN

- The 2016 Dirty Dozen includes the following produce. These are considered among the year's most important produce to buy organic:

Strawberries	Spinach
Apples	Tomatoes
Nectarines	Bell peppers
Peaches	Cherry tomatoes
Celery	Cucumbers
Grapes	Kale/collard greens
Cherries	Hot peppers

- *The Dirty Dozen list contains two additional itemskale/collard greens and hot peppers-because they tend to contain trace levels of highly hazardous pesticides.*

THE CLEAN FIFTEEN

- The least critical to buy organically are the Clean Fifteen list. The following are on the 2016 list:

Avocados	Papayas
Corn	Kiw
Pineapples	Eggplant
Cabbage	Honeydew
Sweet peas	Grapefruit
Onions	Cantaloupe
Asparagus	Cauliflower
Mangos	

- *Some of the sweet corn sold in the United States are made from genetically engineered (GE) seedstock. Buy organic varieties of these crops to avoid GE produce.*

Printed in Great Britain
by Amazon

16517974R00045